# THE INTRODUCTION OF SOCIALISM

# INTO CHINA

Occasional Papers
of the East Asian Institute
Columbia University

# THE CONTEMPORARY CHINA STUDIES PROGRAM OF THE EAST ASIAN INSTITUTE, COLUMBIA UNIVERSITY

The East Asian Institute was established by Columbia University in 1949 to prepare graduate students for careers dealing with East Asia and to aid research and publication on East Asia during the modern period.

Under its aegis the Contemporary China Studies Program was organized in 1959, with the support of the Ford Foundation, for the purpose of advancing the study of contemporary China. The program's activities include support of advanced graduate work, particularly at the doctoral and post-doctoral level, individual research by faculty and visiting scholars, research projects, research conferences, and the publication of scholarly works on contemporary China.

# THE INTRODUCTION
# OF SOCIALISM
# INTO CHINA

## Li Yu-ning

COLUMBIA UNIVERSITY PRESS

New York and London

1971

ISBN: 0-231-03541-1

Library of Congress Catalog Card Number
75-143692

The East Asian Institute
Columbia  University
New York, N.Y.
Printed in the United States of America

# FOREWORD

This study by Dr. Li Yu-ning (Berna-
dette to many of her friends) touches
upon a number of topics of interest to
historians of modern China, but I wish
only to mention two. One is the extent
to which the outlook and social philosophy of Chinese intellectuals has changed
during the past three-quarters of a century. The second is China's debt to Japan in the earlier stages of modernization. An aspect of the changing outlook
and of the debt to Japan was China's introduction to socialism.

Those who introduced socialist thought
to their fellow Chinese intellectuals
were such important figures in the re-
formist and revolutionary decade before
1911 as Liang Ch'i-ch'ao, Wu Chung-yao,
Chu Chih-hsin, Hu Han-min, Feng Tzu-yu,
Sung Chiao-jen, Liao Chung-k'ai, and other polemicists writing in Japan. Dr. Li
has explored the journals in which they
wrote and presents a distillation of the
early conceptions of socialism transmitted
to a generation of youths who later became
leaders of twentieth century China. Liang
Ch'i-ch'ao's role was seminal. Sun Yat-
sen's pro-socialist viewpoint is well
known, but it was his younger associates
who expounded socialist ideas somewhat
more systematically than he. Dr. Li's
study helps to clarify what both sides
in a great debate knew and argued. Her
study also helps, in part, to explain
the receptivity towards Marxism and

Leninism among some teachers and their students during the May Fourth period. Socialism was acceptable, even becoming fashionable, as a political philosophy, thanks partly to the work of the Chinese pioneers whom Dr. Li calls to our attention. Their interest in socialism, however, was only one of many interests and their introductory work only one strand in the complex web of intellectual history.

China's recent indebtedness to Japan tends to be overlooked or even obscured for several reasons which need not be detailed here. When Japan showed what modernization could accomplish, many Chinese turned to Japan as teacher, just as others had earlier turned to England and as many later turned to Soviet Russia. From Japan they learned a great variety of fields, such as military science, law, educational reform, medicine, etc. Eagerly acquiring information from every quarter, some Chinese intellectuals discovered from Japanese academic Marxists and from reform socialists an unfamiliar but exciting body of western political thought. This is not surprising; it has been pointed out by various historians. The Russian role, apparently, was negligible at the beginning. Dr. Li has demonstrated explicitly what some of the Japanese channels of information were, and also some of the imperfections of knowledge about European socialism that resulted from this indirect acquaintanceship. This is one more interesting example of the way in which Japan served, early in this century, to widen Chinese intellectual horizons.

C. Martin Wilbur

Professor of Chinese
   History

Columbia University

December 7, 1969

# CONTENTS

# THE INTRODUCTION OF SOCIALISM

## INTO CHINA

# 1. INTRODUCTION

A commonplace of the voluminous Chinese Communist works on the May 4th period published before the Cultural Revolution was a reference to the introduction of Marxism and the invariable quotation from Mao Tse-tung: "It was through the Russians that the Chinese found Marxism. Before the October Revolution, the Chinese were not only ignorant of Lenin and Stalin, they did not even know of Marx and Engels. The salvoes of the October Revolution brought us Marxism-Leninism."[1]

The present paper demonstrates that Mao's view in this regard is open to interpretation. Thousands of Chinese intellectuals came to know the names of Marx and Engels at the beginning of this century. There then took place what may be regarded as the earliest discussions on the nature of Chinese society from a Marxist standpoint and the anticipation of several recurrent themes in later controversies. Chinese thinking was stimulated by Japanese rather than Russian sources, a salient point in part evidenced by the widespread adoption of Japanese translations of Marxist terminology, most of which are current to this day.

This view may be substantiated by a survey of essential Chinese materials

1

pertaining to socialism published between the late nineteenth and the early twentieth centuries, that is to say, from the first introduction of Western socialist concepts to the conclusion of the historical controversy between the Min-pao (People's Journal) and the Hsin-min ts'ung-pao (New People's Miscellany) on the question of social revolution in China. Moreover, this survey may also convey a knowledge of Chinese writers' understanding of socialism by the year 1907.

2

# 2. THE INITIAL STAGE

It is extremely difficult to state with exactitude when Chinese intellectuals first became acquainted with European socialist ideas in general, or Marxist doctrines in particular. However, by the beginning of this century many Chinese scholars who had been exposed to "Western learning" were beginning to acquire some knowledge of socialism.

## Yen Fu and K'ang Yu-wei

As is well known, Chinese students began to study in Europe and the United States during the early seventies of last century. Possibly some of them had contact with the ideas of Western socialism. But the vast majority of them studied sciences and technology, and they have left us no record of the extent of their knowledge of socialism. The one exception is Yen Fu (1854-1921), the famous translator and advocate of social Darwinism, who studied naval science in England during 1877-1879. Although as early as 1890 the North China Herald of Shanghai published articles on activities of European social revolutionaries,[2] the first Chinese reference to Western socialism seems to be in an essay by Yen Fu,

3

entitled "Yüan ch'iang" written in 1895.
In this essay, Yen noted that scientific
progress in the West had led to extreme
economic inequality, which in turn gave
rise to what he called "the parties for
the equalization of the rich and the
poor" (chün p'in fu chih tang), probably
a reference to socialist parties.[3]

Like his contemporary Yen Fu, K'ang
Yu-wei (1858-1927) was also sensitive
to the widening gap between the rich
and the poor in the West.  In the Ta-
t'ung shu (The Book of the Great
Community), which was completed in 1902,
K'ang made a diagnosis of the capitalist
industrial system:

> With regard to the struggle between
> labor and capital: in recent years
> they have become more intense, be-
> cause of machines  being used to
> make things and completely replacing
> the artisan.... But men who have
> the ability to set up the machines
> of large factories must necessarily
> be big capitalists.  Hence nowadays
> the large factory, the large railway
> or shipbuilding shop, the large
> emporium, and the large farm--all
> are run by big capitalists.  A
> thousand or ten thousand laborers
> depend upon one factory or shop for
> their living, while the capitalist
> can fix wages as he sees fit, control-
> ling and exploiting the laborers.
> Whereby the rich become richer and
> the poor become poorer.[4]

Like Yen Fu, K'ang Yu-wei saw economic disparity as the reason for the emergence of schools of socialism. The two men even shared a similarity in terminology. In the essay "Yüan ch'iang" Yen referred to Herbert Spencer's sociology as ch'ün hsüeh (literally, study of groups) and to schools of socialism as "parties for the equalization of the rich and the poor." K'ang rendered socialist doctrines as jen-ch'ün chih shuo (literally, theories concerning human groups or society) and communist ideas as chün-ch'an chih shuo (literally, theories for the equalization of property).[5] K'ang wrote:

> In recent years there has been a sudden rise of struggles by labor unions to coerce the capitalists in Europe and America. This is only the beginning. The formation of labor unions will certainly increase in the future. One fears that this will lead to the calamity of bloody conflicts.... A hundred years hence it will certainly draw the attention of the entire world. Therefore nowadays socialist and communist doctrines are gaining increasing popularity, which will constitute a most important subject of discussion.[6]

However, K'ang Yu-wei recognized that economic inequalities had existed in the pre-industrial age, not only in the West, but also in the East. In his estimate, economic inequalities in

Asia stemmed primarily from the fact
that there was not enough arable land
and that "people could buy and sell
land." The well-field system was based
on the principle: "with equality,
without poverty." However, it could be
implemented only in earlier stages of
civilization. Wang Mang's equal land
policy failed miserably.[7] In the West,
"the Englishman [sic] Mr. Fu [François
M. C. Fourier, 1772-1837] in his theory
of livelihood wanted to support [a group
of] a thousand persons by means of a
large 'well-field' of ten [square] li.
His idea was very jen, but also
impractical."[8] According to K'ang, all
these measures failed because they did
not get at the root of economic ills--
the institution of private ownership of
property.[9]

Professor Kung-chuan Hsiao has
pointed out that there is "a clear note
of socialism"[10] in the Ta-t'ung shu
and that "the reference to Fourier
constitutes definite proof that K'ang
had come into contact with socialist
ideas" by 1902. But K'ang's knowledge
of socialism was "quite hazy and
fragmentary."[11] Nevertheless, K'ang
was "an outstanding forerunner of the
socialist movement in modern China."[12]
It is impossible to ascertain precisely
when and where K'ang acquired his
knowledge of socialism. Professor
Hsiao feels that K'ang learned of it
"probably for the first time during
his short sojourn in Japan"[13] after the
collapse of the Hundred Days' Reform.

6

As K'ang wrote the Ta-t'ung-shu when socialism was "in the air," "it is hardly
surprising that socialistic sentiments
colored the utopian thought of a man who
ever since 1879 had made efforts to ac-
quaint himself with 'Western learning.'"[14]
In any case, K'ang's knowledge of socialism could not have come directly from
Russian sources, for he could not read
Russian.

Despite its importance as a milestone
in China's socialist thinking, the Ta-
t'ung-shu had little influence on the development of socialist currents in the
early twentieth century, for its first
two portions were not published until
1919 and the complete book was not released until the mid-1930s.[15]


Liang Ch'i-ch'ao

The man who first acquainted the Chinese
reader with socialist ideas was K'ang Yu-
wei's most prominent follower, Liang Ch'i-
ch'ao (1873-1929) who, by general consen-
sus, had greater influence upon Chinese
intellectual development than any other
individual during the period between 1898
and 1905. Quite possibly, Liang first
encountered socialist ideas through his
extensive reading in Japanese on various
subjects shortly after his flight to
Japan following the failure of the reform movement of 1898. Scalapino and
Schiffrin have stated: "Liang wrote what

7

was probably the first article on socialism in Chinese in the <u>Ch'ing-i pao</u> in 1899."[16]  We know that in 1899 Liang wrote an essay entitled "Lun ch'iang-ch'üan" (On Power), saying that the proletariat's revolution against the power of the capitalists and the women's revolution against the power of men were "two inevitable things." "After these two revolutions," he said, "everybody would possess power, thus reaching the summit of power, which is called grand peace."[17]

By 1901, Liang Ch'i-ch'ao had learned more about socialism, and meanwhile the Japanese influence on him had grown more marked.  Japanese translations of Western terminology, as he admitted himself, studded his writings,[18] and even his literary style carried a Japanese flavor.[19]  Terms such as "socialism" (<u>she-hui chu-i</u>, or <u>shakai shugi</u>), "capitalist" (<u>tzu-pen-chia</u>, or <u>shihonka</u>) and a host of others had become part of his vocabulary; and mainly due to Liang's introduction, innumerable Japanese terms entered the Chinese language.[20]  Like K'ang Yu-wei, Liang was quick to recognize the potential of socialism.  He wrote in 1902 an essay entitled "Kan-she yü fang-jen" (Inter-ference and Laissez-faire):

From ancient times to the present, there have been only two main theories concerning ways of governing: interference and laissez-faire....

8

The trend of free competition led
to the thriving of monopoly. The
rich became richer, the poor became
poorer. As a result, modern socialism arose. Socialism appears
as if it were for out-and-out
laissez-faireism; actually it is
for interference. It will put together human groups like a machine
and move them around with an over-
all switch. It seeks equality amid
inequalities. It is clear that socialism will reach everywhere in
the 20th century. Therefore, I say
that the 20th century is an age for
the complete triumph of interference.[21]

By 1902, Liang Ch'i-ch'ao had definitely heard of the name of Marx, which he
transliterated as Mai-k'e-shih. In an
article entitled "Chin-hua-lun ke-ming-
che Chi-te chih hsüeh-shuo" (The Theory of
Kidd, the Revolutionary Evolutionist),
Liang identified Marx as "the Mount T'ai
and the Dipper of German socialism." He
further quoted Benjamin Kidd as saying:
"There are two most influential schools
of thought in present-day Germany: Marx's
socialism and Nietzsche's individualism.
... Marx said that the ills of present-day
society lay in the fact that the weak majority have been suppressed by the strong
minority."[22] In another article written
in 1903, Liang said: "Marx, the founder
of socialism, was a German and author of
many books."[23] He had also heard of the
name Lassalle (La-shih-so-erh) and the

9

theory that all capital was plunder. Liang wrote in 1904 in an article called "Chung-kuo chih she-hui chu-i" (Chinese Socialism):

> Socialism is a special product of the world of the last hundred years. Its essence is no more than public ownership of land and capital and the notion that labor is the exclusive source of value of everything. Marx had said that contemporary economic society was actually formed by the minority who have stolen the land of the majority. Lassalle said that landlords and capitalists, without exception, were thieves and robbers. These arguments are quite exciting to hear. Yet, they existed in China in the past. [Then Liang cited an edict issued by Wang Mang and a quotation from Su Hsün, a famous poet and essayist of the Sung dynasty.] How similar these statements sound to the Declaration of the International Federation of Working Men in 1866! [sic] The well-field system in ancient China was indeed based on the same principle as modern socialism.[24]

By 1904, some of Liang Ch'i-ch'ao's basic views about socialism began to take shape and they constituted a basis for his debates with the Min-pao group in the following years. An article written in that year and published in the Hsin-min ts'ung-pao, entitled "Wai-tzu shu-ju wen-

t'i" (The Problem of the Inflow of
Foreign Capital), shows that he had come
to grasp an important tenet of Marxism:
that capital was the key to economy and
society. Liang opened his discourse with
a striking thesis--the imperialism (ti-
kuo chu-i, or teikoku shugi) of the
powers stemmed from the fact that surplus
capital had to find markets in unindus-
trialized countries such as India and
China. He then divided foreign capital
into three categories: (1) loans to government, (2) loans to either public or
private financial organizations, and (3)
foreign investment independent of local
government or organizations. He maintained that foreign capital in China be-
longed largely to the third category,
which was harmful to China's economy. In
his opinion, the most disadvantageous
loans were those to railway, mining, and
other large industrial enterprises.
While recognizing the need for foreign
capital to industrialize China, he feared
that foreign capital would bring to China
the social ills that had plagued the West.
Since the Industrial Revolution, the rich
had become richer and the poor poorer.
The gap which formerly separated the nobility and the commoners had been replaced by that between two sharply divided
classes (chieh-chi, or kaikyū): the extremely rich minority and the extremely
poor majority. The primary driving force
for the deterioration of Western society
was capital, and hence socialists had
considered public ownership of capital

11

as the most important task. "Where there
is capital, there is happiness." With
the enormous inflow of foreign capital,
foreign capitalists would constitute
the rich minority class while the
Chinese would become the extremely poor
majority class. This would mean the
deprivation of the Chinese people's
happiness. Moreover, the extensive
power of large foreign capitalists
would stifle small Chinese capitalists
and landowners. However, Liang did not
flatly reject utilization of foreign
capital. Rather, he proposed that the
future new government, when established,
raise a large foreign loan to develop
large industries and follow the
principles of state socialism (kuo-chia
she-hui chu-i, or kokka shakai shugi) of
Germany and Austria, such as nationalization of railways. He hoped that these
measures would prevent the occurrence in
China of the social ills which had
existed in the West and that they might
enable China to become an industrial
model for other nations to follow. As
regards nationalization of capital,
Liang considered it a universal principle
(shih-chieh chih kung-li). But it had
not yet been realized in the advanced
West, and therefore it definitely could
not be applied to contemporary China.[25]


Earliest Chinese Books on Socialism

Not only did Liang Ch'i-ch'ao introduce
socialist ideas and terms through his

own prolific and popular writings in the Hsin-min ts'ung-pao, he was probably instrumental in the publication of the earliest Chinese books dealing with socialism. In 1901, together with other constitutionalists, he founded in Shanghai a publishing house, the Kuang-chih shu-chü (Extension of Knowledge Book Company),[26] which later proved to be worthy of its name. Apart from other translations, this Book Company published in 1903 translations of three Japanese books on socialism, namely: (1) Fukui Junzō, Kinsei shakai shugi (Modern Socialism; Tokyo, 1899), translated into Chinese by Chao Pi-chen under the title Chin-shih she-hui chu-i; (2) Nishikawa Kōjirō, Shakaitō (The Socialist Party; Tokyo, 1901), translated by Chou Pai-kao under the title She-hui tang; (3) Murai Chishi, Shakai shugi (Socialism; Tokyo, 1899) translated by Lo Ta-wei under the title She-hui chu-i.[27]

Of the three books, the first and the third are not available to us.[28] However, we may get an inkling of the first book by Fukui Junzō through references to it in other works. The translation was divided into four sections. The second section, entitled "German Socialism," deals principally with Karl Marx (Chia-lu Ma-lu k'o-ssu) and his theory. It is quoted as saying that socialism prior to Marx was "talks of pure imagination." Only Marx's socialism was "based on profound

13

academic principles and thorough research and it discovered truth and justice through studies of economic laws. Therefore, it could easily be practiced among the majority proletariat (lao-min) and win wide support and approval.... Even those who disliked socialist theories found it difficult to refute his theory." The fourth section, dealing with "The Contemporary Situation of Socialist Parties in the Countries of Europe and America," said that "The International Federation of Working Men organized by Marx had become the center of control for the contemporary socialist movement."29

That Liang Ch'i-ch'ao and other constitutional reformers were not the only ones whose attention was attracted by socialism is suggested by the fact that there were other Chinese publications dealing with socialism. In 1902, Chao Pi-chen, the same translator of Kinsei shakai shuqi, published a translation of a book by the renowned Japanese socialist Kōtoku Shūsui under the title Erh-shih shih-chi chih kuai-wu ti-kuo chu-i (Niju seiki no kaibutsu teikoku shuqi, Imperialism, the Specter of the Twentieth Century; T'ung-ya Book Company in Shanghai). Kinsei shakai shuqi by Murai Chishi had at least two Chinese translations: one just mentioned, the other translated by Hou T'ai-wan and published by Wen-ming Book Company in the same year of 1903. An advertisement of Murai's book appeared in the widely

14

read Su-pao (Kiangsu Daily News) of
Shanghai. Shimada Saburō's Shakai shugi
gaihyo (General Critique of Socialism) was
translated and published under the title
She-hui chu-i kai-p'ing by the Tso-hsin
Company in 1903.30

Earliest Chinese Journals on Socialism

Apart from the Hsin-min ts'ung-pao, before
1905 there were at least three other Chinese journals providing some information
on Western socialism. They were the
Shih-wu pao (Current Affairs), the I-shu
hui-pien (Collected Translations), and
the Hsin shih-chieh hsüeh-pao (New World).
The former two were printed in Japan but
also circulated in mainland China; the
last was of Shanghai. Founded on 9 August 1896 by Huang Tsun-hsien, Wang K'ang-
nien, and Liang Ch'i-ch'ao, the Shih-wu
pao, which carried the English subtitle
"The Chinese Progress," was a most important journal published by the constitutionalists during the period of the 1898
Reform Movement. It consisted of several
sections dealing with editorials, imperial decrees, current events, and translations of excerpts from foreign newspapers.
The section of translations from newspapers occupied half the space of the
journal, mainly from English and Japanese
sources. The I-shu hui-pien, which carried the English subtitle "A Monthly Magazine of Translated Political Works," was
the earliest periodical organized by
Chinese students in Japan. Beginning
publication in Tokyo on 6 December 1900,
it was the journal of a noted Chinese

students' organization in Japan, the I-shu Hui-pien She (Society for Collected Translations) founded in 1900. A monthly of about fifty pages, the journal translated numerous works of social and political science. It also published some of its translations in book form, which enjoyed considerable popularity. Original authors of the works translated were of various nationalities, including German, French, American, English, and Japanese; the Chinese translations were mostly, if not invariably, based on Japanese versions.

As early as 1896, the Shih-wu pao carried a news item translated from the Japanese newspaper Kokumin Shimpō on the third Congress of the Second International convened in London. The event was referred to as the "international conference" (wan-kuo ta-hui, bankoku taigai) of the "socialist parties" (she-hui tang, shakaitō). The Congress was reported to have discussed the public school system and international disarmament and to have voted on the prohibition of children under the age of 18 working at night in factories and on the limit of 24 working hours per week.[31] In 1898 the same Shih-wu pao translated from the Japanese daily Ōsaka Asahi a news item on the political parties in Germany. It provided statistics on the number of seats that each German party had in the parliament and of its votes to the parliament. The Reform Socialist Party (Keng-ke she-hui tang) was reported to have 13 seats in the parliament and 263,861 votes, while the Social Democratic Party (She-hui

16

min-cheng tang) had 45 parliamentary
seats and 1,786,738 votes.[32]

During 1900-1901 the I-shu hui-pien
published serially a translation with
the title "Chin-shih cheng-chih shih"
(History of Contemporary Politics) written by Ariga Nagao. In it the German
"Socialist Party" (She-hui-tang) was
described as a party which stood against
the monarchical polity, capitalism, and
the Church. According to it, the German
"Socialist Party" consisted of two factions, one led by Marx (Mai-k'e-ssu) and
the other by Lassalle (La-ssu-lai).
Prior to 1848 both Marx and Lassalle had
already won followers by advocating "lib-
erty" (tzu-yu, jiyū), although the two
men's theories were different. Marx
reportedly propagated the idea of "equalization of wealth" (chün-fu chih shuo)
during his journalist career in Cologne
and consequently, after being expelled
from Germany, sought refuge in London.
There he directed the General Council of
the First International, that is, the
"International Federation of Working Men"
(Wan-kuo kung-jen tsung-hui), which
aimed to emancipate the workers from the
yoke of the capitalists. The article
told also that Marx's pupils Wilhelm
Liebknecht and August Bebel founded the
Arbeiterbund, which became affiliated
with the International in 1868.

According to the same article, the
Lassalleans had nothing to do with the

17

First International and the group led by
Bebel and Liebknecht. Lassalle was not
a radical, but a far-sighted statesman
and patriot. He entered into negotia-
tions with Bismarck in order to protect
the workers. He considered the alliance
of the workers and bourgeoisie as futile
and preferred to work through the State
with a view to obtaining universal
suffrage. In 1863 he founded the
Federation of All German Workers.
Bismarck frequently praised Lassalle,
but Bebel and Liebknecht charged
Lassalle with selling-out "socialism"
(she-hui-chu-i) to the government.
Following Lassalle's death in a duel in
1864, the leadership of the Federation
of All German Workers passed to Johann
von Schweitzer.

It is interesting to note the
anonymous translator's commentary on
socialism. "Out of their grief over
the disparity between the rich and the
poor and the oppression imposed on the
laborers by the capitalists, some Western scholars advocated the theory of
equalizing the properties of the rich
and the poor. This is called socialism.
The reason why [the theory] refers to
society is that it has plans for all,
not just for one person or one family.
The well-field system of ancient China
is socialism."[33]

In early 1903, the Hsin shih-chieh
hsüeh-pao published in installments a
long essay by Tu Shih-chen discussing

Hisamatsu Yoshinori's <u>Kinsei shakai shugi hyōron</u> (A Critique of Modern Socialism).[34] The journal is unavailable at the present time.

The above exposition should be sufficient to indicate that by 1905 such foreign names as "socialism" and Marx were no longer total strangers to many Chinese readers. Those who had made acquaintance with them were not restricted to overseas students and exiles, but included dwellers in mainland China as well, since the <u>Shih-wu pao</u>, the <u>I-shu hui-pien</u>, the <u>Hsin shih-chieh hsüeh-pao</u>, the <u>Hsin-min ts'ung pao</u>, and books by Liang Ch'i-ch'ao enjoyed wide circulation in the interior.[35] Moreover, several books on socialism were published within China's borders. While the extent and quality of Chinese knowledge of socialist theories is uncertain, there is no doubt that Chinese knew of Marx before 1905.

The foregoing facts also make it evident that Chinese ventures into the study of socialist ideas were inspired by Japanese, not Russian, writers. Martin Bernal has pointed out that the Japanese socialist movement, which antedated the Chinese by several years, started in the late 1890s and originated from two sources: the Christian and the liberal. Japanese Christian Socialists had been under the influence of American missionaries, "many of whom were concerned about the 'social

19

problem'--the problem of increasing
poverty under capitalism--which appeared to contemporaries to be particularly
severe in the United States during the
last decades of the nineteenth century."36  We have already seen that
both K'ang Yu-wei and Liang Ch'i-ch'ao
were very concerned with the same "social problem," and we shall see later
that many Chinese shared their concern.
It is perhaps significant to note that
in 1903 a Chinese translation of a
Japanese work was published under the
title She-hui wen-t'i (Social Problem).
Noteworthy also is the fact that among
the earliest Chinese books on socialism
was the translation of Shakaito by
Nishikawa Kōjirō, a prominent Christian
Socialist.37  The name of Kōtoku
Shūsui, perhaps the most influential
Japanese socialist of the liberal
brand, appeared in the Chinese press
even earlier. As just mentioned, a
Chinese translation of Kōtoku's Imperialism, the Specter of the Twentieth
Century was published in 1902.  Liang
Ch'i-ch'ao certainly knew of Kōtoku, to
whom he referred in his writings.
Further research must ascertain whether
Liang was indebted to Kōtoku for his
interpretation of "imperialism." A book
under the title Imperialism (Teikoku
shugi) by Ukita Kazuomi, an apologist of
expansionism, was translated into Chinese
as early as 1895. It interpreted imperialism as an outlet for surplus capital.
Harold Z. Schiffrin says: "Both Liang
Ch'i-ch'ao and the young intellectuals

20

whom he first inspired were probably influenced by Japanese literature on imperialism." Liang was not alone in expounding imperialism, there were many other articles on the same subject in Chinese journals of the time.[38]

An incident may well illustrate Chinese interest in socialism. In 1902 some former students of the Nan-yang Kung-hsüeh expressed the idea of establishing a socialist organization.[39] However, it is not known whether their idea was transformed into reality or whether there existed a Chinese socialist study group before 1907. Nevertheless, the adventure into the realm of socialist theories had broadened the Chinese intellectual horizon, and more important, it had opened an avenue for later scholars to draw inspiration and information from the readily accessible Japanese sources.

# 3. THE YEARS 1905-1907--CONTROVERSY BETWEEN THE MIN-PAO AND THE HSIN-MIN TS'UNG-PAO

If the Chinese first encountered so-cialist ideas mainly through the publica-tions of the constitutionalists, they possibly learned more about them from the writings of the T'ung-meng Hui members, a fact that the Kuomintang historians have preferred not to emphasize. Min-pao, the official organ of the T'ung-meng Hui, was one of the most important media through which socialist theories were disseminat-ed among Chinese revolutionaries, and its lively controversy with the constitution-al reformers, which was a major event in modern Chinese political-intellectual history, served to stimulate the interest of Chinese intellectuals in general in the subject of socialism.

The Min-pao's controversy with the constitutionalists (mainly Liang Ch'i-ch'ao) was only a part of the great debate for a broader program relating to China's future. The inauguration of the Min-pao in 1905 found the two camps pitted against each other in polemical warfare. At first, controversy cen-tered around the necessity for racial revolt, that is, the overthrow of the Manchus, and the possibility of simul-taneous action at both the racial and

political levels. Following this stage,
Sun Yat-sen's theory of political tute-
lege became the theme of controversy,
while the last round was reserved for
the issue of the need for a social
revolution.[40]

Though it reached its climax in the
years of 1905-07, the controversy between
the Sun Yat-sen and Liang Ch'i-ch'ao
groups on socialism can be traced to 1900
when the two men unsuccessfully attempted
to work out a program of cooperation.
"Nationalization of land" was reportedly
an issue on which they disagreed.[41] It
is uncertain as to the precise date of
Sun's first encounter with socialist
ideas; probably it was in 1897-98 when he
was in Europe. Nor do we know exactly
when he first put forth "equalization of
land rights," which according to the Min-
pao writers was equivalent to "nationalization of land," as one of his political
principles. Available data show that
equalization of land rights was included
in the oath of a branch of the Hsing-
Chung Hui in Hanoi, which he founded in
late 1902. The same term appeared in the
oath of the Revolutionary Military Academy established by him in Japan in 1903.
The "New Regulations Governing the Chih-
kung-t'ang," which he reorganized in San
Francisco in 1904, stated that equalization of land rights was one of the goals
of the organization.[42] By 1905, Sun and
his followers had called themselves
social revolutionaries, and the newly
established T'ung-meng Hui upheld the

equalization of land rights as one of its four basic principles. The min-sheng chu-i, which the Min-pao group used interchangeably with shakai shugi, was essentially Henry George's doctrine of the single tax system and the appropriation of the unearned increase of land values. According to Sun and his followers, it was an effective preventive for the economic inequities which characterized Western capitalist countries.

## Chu Chih-hsin

Chu Chih-hsin (1885-1920), one of Sun Yat-sen's faithful followers, was the first to bring Marxism to the forum of the Min-pao. In the opinion of Scalapino and Schiffrin, Chu appeared "to have been one of the most sophisticated" of the early socialist thinkers in Sun's group, "having pioneered in the effort to understand the trends in Western socialism."[43] Under the pen name Che-shen, Chu published in the second and third issues of the Min-pao a by now famous article entitled "Te-i-chih she-hui ke-ming-chia hsiao-chuan" (Short Biographies of German Social Revolutionaries).[44] He advanced the view that social forces evolved toward change, which in turn dictated political adjustment. Revolution resulted from the inability of political forces to consolidate social adjustment. Political and social problems could only be solved together if these problems existed simultaneously. This, said Chu, was a

24

new discovery of many European socialist thinkers. He further noted that the socialist movement had been most thriving in Germany where the socialist party had become a political force because it had won a few parliamentary seats. Election to parliament he considered as the first step for the implementation of socialist policy.

In the same article Chu Chih-hsin provided biographical sketches of Marx and Lassalle and summaries of their theories in the hope that this information might become widely known to the Chinese and serve as a basis for the propagation of a social revolution. He said: "The theory of Ma-erh-k'e [Marx] that capital is plunder fits extremely well any discussion of capital at the present times." He lauded the Communist Manifesto as the first socialist document to offer a satisfactory interpretation and solution of capital, quoting it in several instances, for example, "the history of all hitherto existing society is the history of class struggles." In his discourse, he translated with footnotes the ten-point program in Section II of the Manifesto, the first such translation in the Chinese language. He further commented: "Marx wrote a considerable amount, often collaborating with Yen-chi-erh [Engels], and scholars valued their works. His academic works, which have been honored by the world particularly, are the History of Capital and Capital. Marx considered that capitalists were those who plundered, acting like thieves and robbers, and that they fattened themselves with the profits gained solely through exploiting the proletariat [lao-tung-che, or rōdōsha]." But Chu had doubts on this point. "Production and consumption do not necessarily match all the time. Sometimes, there is surplus, people think of insufficiency, therefore there is such a thing as saving, a fact that has existed since the age of isolated economy. To use savings for the purpose of production increase is the beginning of capital. In which case, the capitalist [tzu-pen-chia] and the worker [lao-tung-che] is one and the same person. How could [capital] be plunder which turned into savings? Therefore, [Marx's theory] may be said to be exaggerated."

Chu Chih-hsin's grasp of Marxist theory is evidenced in his other Min-pao articles, for example, "Lun she-hui ke-ming tang yü cheng-chih ke-ming ping hsing" (Why the Social Revolution Should Be Carried Out Simultaneously with the Political Revolution).[45] This article was intended to refute the charges made by Liang Ch'i-ch'ao against the T'ung-meng Hui's social program, that land nationalization was a stratagem to woo the lower stratum of society and was liable to create internal chaos, which would then provide the excuse for foreign intervention. Chu's reply was that land nationalization would be carried out by legal and gradual means which would not lead to turmoil and that the T'ung-meng Hui did not intend to

26

seize the wealth of the rich and divide it among the poor. Although in China disparity between the rich and the poor was not as great as in the West, a laissez-faire competitive system and the absolute recognition of private property had come into existence. Therefore, it was desirable to plan institutional restrictions on further concentration of wealth at the time of the political revolution. It would be easy to carry out a social revolution for two reasons, Chu averred. First, the gap between the rich and the poor was not yet great and "the spirit of plundering capital" did not yet flourish. Second, the Chinese people were familiar with policies for curbing the rich and the many attempts to do so by former governments. By implication, Chu felt that socialist ideas were a part of China's heritage and that socialism was a preventive rather than a cure because capitalism had not arrived in China. In holding these views, Chu was essentially no different from K'ang Yu-wei, Liang Ch'i-ch'ao, Sun Yat-sen, and a host of other contemporaries.

Chu Chih-hsin wrote two other articles in the Min-pao touching upon socialism, namely, "Ying-kuo hsin tsung-hsüan-chü lao-tung-che chih chin-pu" (The Progress of the Proletariat in the Recent British General Election),[46] and "Ts'ung she-hui chu-i lun t'ieh-tao kuo-yu chi Chung-kuo t'ieh-tao chih kuan-pan ssu-pan" (Discussion From a Socialist Viewpoint of

Railway Nationalization and Official and Private Management of China's Railways).[47] The first article enthusiastically reported the news that in a recent general election the British Labour Party had won forty-nine seats, an increase of forty-eight seats compared to the previous election. Chu noted that traditionally the British Labour Party had been inactive in politics, and he speculated that its recent active participation in the election was motivated by a desire to emulate the German Social Democratic Party. With the present speed of progress, Chu hoped, the British Labour Party might become the majority party in England within the next ten years.

"Discussion from a Socialist Viewpoint of Railway Nationalization and Official and Private Management of China's Railways" was meant to justify the T'ung-meng Hui's program of railway nationalization. That which appeared in the Min-pao was only the first part of an intended longer article, but for reasons unknown, the remainder was never published. Apart from the introduction, the published article is devoted to introducing theories concerning nationalization or government ownership of railways. Chu's sources were all in Japanese: Richard T. Ely's Outline of Economics translated by Yamauchi Masaaki under the title Keizaigaku gairon; Takimoto Yoshio, Kakakunō zaiseigaku (Wagner's Theory of Finance); Kobayashi Usaburō, Hikaku zaisei-

28

gaku (Theory of Comparative Finance); and a few essays by Japanese authors published in the journal Kokka gakkai zasshi (National Academy Magazine).

Chu Chih-hsin was probably the most sophisticated socialist thinker among Sun Yat-sen's group and also quite possibly the T'ung-meng Hui's most competent strategist on economic and financial matters, authoring nearly all the major articles on these subjects in the Min-pao. It is pertinent to inquire how Chu acquired his knowledge of the social sciences. The answer is found in his educational background, ideas, vocabulary, and the references indicated by his writings.

Before going to Japan in 1904, Chu Chih-hsin had studied the Chinese classics and mathematics in Kwangtung. After arriving in Tokyo he specialized in economics at a school called Fa-cheng shu-ch'eng k'o which had a one-year program specially designed for Chinese students. As far as we know, Japanese was the only language required in this school. Apart from his aptitude in other subjects, Chu was known for his linguistic talents and was said to have mastered Japanese within a year. Thus, his educational background suggests that most likely his knowledge of Western socialism came through Japanese sources.[48]

While Chu Chih-hsin might be considered original on a number of points in interpreting Chinese history and revolution in Marxian terms, for instance, that peasants were a revolutionary force,[49] nevertheless several ideas expressed in his writings suggest Japanese influence. In both the articles "Short Biographies of German Social Revolutionaries" and "The Progress of the Proletariat in the Recent British General Election," he maintained that socialist parties could and should gradually ascend to power through parliamentary means--a concept held by European social democrats and by some American Christian socialists, whose writings the Japanese had translated in the late 1890s. Richard Ely enjoyed a special popularity among Japanese intellectuals and several of his books were translated at the turn of the century.[50] Chu Chih-hsin referred to Ely several times in his article on the nationalization of railways. Not only Chu, but the Min-pao group as well as Liang Ch'i-ch'ao relied heavily on Ely as a source of information on socialism. Secondly, as remarked above, Chu had the highest regard for the German Social Democratic Party among all the socialist parties. Traditionally, a large number of the Japanese were German-oriented, and it was a common trait for many Japanese socialists to consider their German counterparts as models.[51]

The most obvious evidence for Chu Chih-hsin's reliance on Japanese sources for his knowledge of socialism was his written terminology. The majority of the

30

terms he used to discuss questions relating to the social sciences can be traced to Japanese origin, and he himself sometimes made it plain that he had followed Japanese translations. Even though in his article "Why the Social Revolution Should Be Carried Out Simultaneously with the Political Revolution" he recommended that the Japanese term shihonka (capitalist) be replaced with a Chinese compound hao-yu, and rōdōsha (proletariat) with hsi-min to include peasants, he resumed using Japanese translations in his later articles in the Min-pao. This seeming inconsistency suggests how heavily Japanese influence had weighed with him. Moreover, his bibliographical references named were all either Japanese works or Japanese translations from English. He might also have read Japanese translations of German works on socialism, for he occasionally provided German equivalents for terms rendered in Chinese characters, a common practice of many Japanese scholars at the time. There is no evidence that Chu derived any of his knowledge of Marxism from Russian sources.


Hu Han-min

Hu Han-min was also an important spokesman for the T'ung-meng Hui and much of his writing had Sun Yat-sen's personal endorsement. Hu's well-known article, entitled "Min-pao chih liu ta chu-i" (The Six Great Principles of the Min-pao),

31

was the first exposition of the general principles of the T'ung-meng Hui.[52] His treatment of the land nationalization question  in the framework of socialism is interesting not so much for his originality as for its repetition of several themes seen in the writings of his contemporaries. First, like K'ang Yu-wei, Liang Ch'i-ch'ao, and many others, Hu saw that economic inequities had given rise to socialist schools, although he expressed the by now familiar idea in his own way. "The ills of modern civilized countries do not lie in the [existence] of political classes, but of the economic classes, and they have given rise to socialism. Although there are various schools of socialism, they share one essential principle, that is, equalization of the economic classes."  In Hu's opinion, socialist schools could be divided into two types: communism (kung-ch'an chu-i), and collectivism (kuo-ch'an chu-i),  and the theory concerning land nationalization was part of collectivism. Only democratic constitutional states were able to practice collectivism because the parliament, which represented the people, could see to it that the government pursued policies fair to all.  The stage of its development prevented China's practicing any form of collectivism, but the ancient well-field system provided a foundation for land nationalization.  Therefore, to carry out land nationalization together with political reform was not a difficult task. Thus,

32

the legend of the well-field system was again used in propagating socialist policies.

To justify land nationalization, Hu Han-min borrowed Henry George's theory that land was created by no man but was the property of everyone like the sunlight and air. He asserted that in the early stage of the landowner system, capital came from labor and savings and was used for production purposes--a point which reminds us of Chu Chih-hsin's critique of the Marxian concept of capital. Later, with the increase of land value resulting from the development of civilization, capitalists (tzu-pen-chia) exploited the proletariat (lao-tung-che) through monopoly of land, and eventually landowners controlled all capital and wealth. By implication, Hu conceived land as capital and landowners as capitalists, and the peasants as proletarians.

Having described the evils brought about through private ownership and land concentration in England, Hu Han-min then struck an optimistic note for solving the land problem in China. The T'ung-meng Hui's program for abolishing private ownership and tenancy of land could successfully create a classless Chinese society through its reinforcement by political revolution, he asserted.

Hu Han-min and Liang Ch'i-ch'ao

Another article by Hu Han-min expounding
socialism was published in the same jour-
nal--"Kao fei-nan min-sheng chu-i che"
(To the Critic of the Min-sheng chu-i).[53]
This long article, running to some 36,000
Chinese characters, was personally en-
dorsed by Sun Yat-sen. Designed to refute
Liang Ch'i-ch'ao's critique of the T'ung-
meng Hui's socialist platform, it is perhaps the most inclusive essay of all the
articles of the same nature in the Min-
pao. Though involving refutation of
essential points of Liang Ch'i-ch'ao's
hitherto expressed criticism of the T'ung-
meng Hui's program, the article was inspired by the publication of a particular
section of an oft-quoted essay by Liang--
"Tsa ta mou pao" (Miscellaneous Answers to
a Certain Journal) appearing in the Hsin-
min ts'ung-pao in serial form. This particular section is entitled "Is a Social
Revolution Needed in Present-Day China?"[54]
Thus, it is well to summarize first
Liang's criticism of the T'ung-meng Hui's
socialist program.

Hu Han-min pointed out that prior to
the publication of the 75th issue of the
Hsin-min ts'ung-pao (23 February 1906),
Liang Ch'i-ch'ao "made great efforts to
introduce socialism to China," and Hu's
charges were probably not unfounded that
the T'ung-meng Hui's advocacy of socialism
accounted for Liang's proclamation in the
75th issue: "This ism has frequently been
able to agitate the lower stratum of
European society." Confronted with a

formidable enemy group who also discussed
one of his favorite subjects, Liang after
1906 naturally found it necessary to re-
view or redefine his views in order to
distinguish himself from his foes. Thus,
his numerous essays written during the
controversy frequently touched upon socialism. An example was "Is a Social
Revolution Needed in Present-Day China?"
the writing of which was prompted by Sun
Yat-sen's October speech in the tenth
issue of the Min-pao (20 December 1906).
Liang's answer to the question was in the
negative.

Liang Ch'i-ch'ao's argument consists
of three essential parts. The first was
that a social revolution was not needed
in China. This theme was built upon the
assumption that due to different historical backgrounds, the economic-social
structure of China was vastly different
from that of Europe. Liang asserted that
social inequities in Europe had pre-industrial origins in the monopoly of land by
the nobility who exploited the majority
peasant-serfs. The industrial revolution,
which led to the concentration of capital
and means of production, only widened the
gap between rich and poor and provided
cause for a social revolution. Liang
quoted from the American economist Richard T. Ely that it was regrettable that
the workers had not organized themselves
into cooperatives, which they might have
done in the early stage of industrialization, and thereby resisted the exploitation of the capitalists. A social revolu-

tion, namely a revolution in distribution, would be a reaction to the industrial revolution, namely a revolution in production. While a social revolution might be necessary or inevitable in Europe, which had suffered from deep-rooted and incurable ills as well as the additional undesirable results of the industrial revolution, the Chinese economy had fared better. Social inequities in China had been less pronounced even when compared to pre-industrial Europe. According to Liang, this was because China had no nobility from the time of the Ch'in dynasty on and there was no church to exploit the peasantry, and because equal inheritance made concentration of wealth difficult. Therefore, China did not have extremely rich and extremely poor classes. Drawing lessons from European experience, when China entered the industrial age, it would experience an evolutionary process and could avoid concentration of capital and means of production by adopting the method of joint stock companies organized by the broad middle class and by taking other preventive measures. Hence, Liang's conclusion was that since China had not been and would not be affected by the problem of distribution, which provided possibilities for a social revolution in Europe, there was no reason for a social revolution in China.

The second part of Liang Ch'i-ch'ao's argument was that a social revolution should not be carried out in China. According to him, the purpose of a social revolution was to achieve equal distribution, that is, to curb the tyranny of the capitalists and to promote the welfare of the proletariat. Although a social revolution might be a most effective cure for European and American ills, it would not be good for China. In his opinion, the primary task for the development of China's economy was "to encourage the capitalists," while "to protect the proletariat" should be only secondary. The reason for this was that native capitalists were needed in order to resist foreign capitalists, who had swarmed into China seeking cheap labor and making use of surplus capital. "If the influence of foreign capitalists were to prevail in our country fully, our four hundred million compatriots would become horses and oxen for all eternity." Should this happen, there would be only two classes in the Chinese economic arena: the foreigners and the Chinese. For the sake of the country, the government should encourage and protect the Chinese capitalists to enable them to expand their enterprises and to compete with foreign capitalists, even at the cost of sacrificing the interest of the proletariat. If the proletariat were encouraged to demand fewer working hours, higher wages, or even to strike, thus causing losses to the Chinese capitalists and weakening their ability to compete with foreign investors, the result might be that the whole country would fall under the control of foreign economic influences. Should this tragedy occur, Liang charged, those who talked about a social revolution would be committing the great sin of destroying the nation.

The third part of Liang Ch'i-ch'ao's argument was that a social revolution could not be carried out in China. This was based on the assumption that if a social revolution was to be carried out at all, it should be a perfect one, or "complete and thorough" (yüan-man) in his own words, otherwise its goals could not be achieved. Yet, even with the present stage of development Europe and America could not achieve a social revolution hundreds of years hence, much less China. Although land nationalization was only a part of socialism, the T'ung-meng Hui maintained that once the land problem was solved, all social problems would be solved and that Europe and America had not been able to solve their social problems because they had not solved the land problem. According to Liang, the highest goal of the "most complete and thorough theory concerning social revolution" was to nationalize all production elements, not just the land. Actually, capital was the most important production element and the primary source of social inequities in the West and determined the land value. Liang therefore argued that if social questions were to be solved, the question of capital had to be solved first   and

38

the land question second. The economic
structure of the new society following a
"most complete and thorough social revolution" could be described in simple
words: the state would be the landowner,
the capitalist, with the citizens as the
proletarians. The state would be like a
company, a unique company which would
take care of everything for the people.

The remainder of Liang's article was
devoted to attacks on Sun Yat-sen's
October speech and Chu Chih-hsin's
article "Why the Social Revolution Should
Be Carried Out Simultaneously with the
Political Revolution." Much of his
criticism is repetitious, although it is
interesting to note Liang's remark that
Sun's brand of socialism was no more than
a revival of the ancient well-field
system. However, Liang said that he was
not against socialism per se and that
actually he was for social reformism,
including state or municipal ownership of
railways, roads, utilities, compulsory
insurance laws, progressive income taxes,
inheritance tax, etc.

As already mentioned, "To the Critic
of Min-sheng chu-i" by Hu Han-min is an
extremely long article. We need only
summarize the essential aspects of Hu's
refutation of Liang's arguments. First,
Hu revealed that although Liang's discussion of Europe's socio-economic
history was based exclusively on
Yamauchi Masaaki's translation of Ely's
Outlines of Economics, Liang purposely

39

avoided mentioning Ely's description
of America. Why? It was because, in
Hu's estimate, Ely's interpretation of
United States economic history did not
suit Liang's theory. According to Ely,
industrialization in Europe was the
outcome of a revolution accompanied by
bloodshed and turmoil, whereas in the
United States it was a peaceful process
of evolution or transition. However,
with the advance of industrialization and
the laissez-faire policy of the government, the rich became richer, and the
proletariat poorer, and hence the
problems of distribution later arose in
the United States. Thus, Hu used Ely's
interpretation to refute Liang. Despite
orderly transition in the beginning of
industrialization, the enormous and
sparsely populated land, and the heritage
of having no oppressive nobility and
church, the United States like Europe had
been facing the possibility of a social
revolution. This meant that even though
America had avoided a revolution in
production, it still might have to face
a revolution in distribution. Then
could Liang say, asked Hu, that China
could avoid a social revolution (revolution in distribution) even if it could
avoid an industrial revolution (revolution in production)? Could the present-
day Chinese economy be favorably compared
with the U.S. economy during its incip-
ient stage of industrialization?

Secondly, Hu Han-min pointed out that
Liang Ch'i-ch'ao's advocacy of protecting

Chinese capitalism contradicted his social reformism aiming to protect the interest of the proletariat. This contra-
diction was due to Liang's fear of the
supremacy of foreign economic power in
China. However, Hu recalled that previ-
ously Liang had maintained that using
foreign capital for production purposes
was beneficial for China, whereas for
consumption it was harmful. Since capitalists from various countries were
eager to have a share in the China market, China would benefit from the international competition while it was impossible for the Chinese financiers with
limited resources to compete successfully
with large foreign capitalists. The im-
port of foreign capital would help to increase production and capital, Hu asserted, and he quoted Ely as saying that capital was the surplus derived from production and used or saved for production
purposes. At the same time, when land
nationalization was realized, the state
would become the large landowner and capitalist, striving for the well-being of
all citizens. Liang himself hoped that
the state would become the landowner and
capitalist, Hu said, so he should actually admire "the socialism advocated by
us." The T'ung-meng Hui's program took
into account the problems of both production and distribution, whereas Liang emphasized production but neglected distribution, a view with which Ely would not
have agreed, said Hu.

Thirdly, Hu Han-min refuted Liang Ch'i-

41

ch'ao's argument that a social revolution could not be carried out in China because it could not yet be carried out in the more advanced Europe and America. Hu replied that Liang "worshipped Europe and America but had no understanding of socialism." According to Hu, modern scholars of socialism invariably admitted that the chance for carrying out socialism in a given country was in inverse proportion to the degree of civilization of that country. A primitive island might be transformed overnight into a socialist paradise, while social problems in Europe and America were deep-rooted and hard to cure. As for China, socialism was a preventive. That Europe and America failed to achieve socialism did not mean that China could not succeed. Liang said that if there should be a social revolution, it should be a "complete and thorough" one. Hu asked what Liang meant by "complete and thorough." There had been various socialist schools contending with one another. School A might accuse school B of being incomplete, while school C might criticize school A as being inadequate. In Hu's opinion, so long as a theory contained no self-contradictions and could fulfill its goals in practice, it could not be regarded as unsatisfactory. Liang had written: "Socialists of various countries had regarded land nationalization as the work to start with; they had not said there was no other work aside from this." Hu retorted: "Have we ever said that there was nothing else besides land nationalization?" Liang was quoted as saying: "[Before the industrial revolution] the land of Europe was already in the hands of a few people, and the capital of Europe was naturally also in the hands of a few people," and "one of the three production elements was already monopolized by a few people, therefore the nobility were at the same time the rich." This was tantamount to a recognition that land was the source of capital, Hu said. If the private ownership of land was not abolished, capitalists were at the same time the landowners and therefore possessed two production elements, namely capital and land, while the proletariat possessed only one, namely labor. Naturally, the proletarians would not be in a position to resist the capitalists. Although in China the class gulf between the rich and the poor was not yet deep because big capitalists had not yet emerged, the land was already in the hands of private individuals. Land nationalization was thus designed to prevent the emergence of the combined capitalist-landowner, to prevent the capitalist-landowners' exploitation of the proletarians. However, the T'ung-meng Hui only intended to nationalize land and large monopolies; it did not propose to nationalize all production elements as Liang proposed. Hu reported that even Marx and Engels permitted ownership of capital by farmers and handicraftsmen.

Liang Ch'i-ch'ao responded to Hu Han-min's long article with a similarly long one which, entitled "Tsai po mou pao chih

43

t'u-ti kuo-yu lun" (A Further Refutation of a Certain Journal's Land Nationalization Doctrine), was published in three installments in the <u>Hsin-min ts'ung-pao</u>.[55] However, instead of continuing the debate on the subject as to whether a social revolution was needed in China, Liang shifted his attention to the land nationalization issue and assaulted with statistics the <u>Min-pao</u>'s fiscal plan for the future. The first of Liang's three-part argument was from the financial viewpoint that land nationalization was unrealistic and impracticable. He said that in England, the land tax was insufficient to cover national expenditures and cited the theory of Kobayashi Usaburō, a Japanese economist, that the larger the country the higher the administrative cost of any government undertakings. China was larger in size than England and hence its expenditure would be higher. Since England could not maintain itself by land tax alone, would it be possible for China to prosper through the single land tax system as the <u>Min-pao</u> claimed? Then Liang questioned the figure of 400 million taels of land tax which the T'ung-meng Hui hoped to collect after the establishment of the new government. Furthermore, was the single tax system a good system? Liang reported that even Adolf Wagner (1835-1917), the eminent German expert on finance who was an advocate of state socialism, maintained that the government should own only part of the industries and leave room for the

44

operation of a private economy. Taxes on private enterprises would provide an important source of national income. In Liang's opinion, nationalization of industries should be carried out gradually. For example, in Japan the railways were at first managed by private industrialists and later taken over by the government. Nationalization was feasible only when there were enough technicians in the country, when the people's regard for public welfare was developed, and when laws and regulations were fully codified. The T'ung-meng Hui's plan to nationalize all large industries upon taking power would lead to undesirable results. To begin with, where could the new government find enough funds to buy all the lands and industries? From the land tax? To believe so was indulging in fantasy. Besides, it would be extremely unfair to the peasants who had to bear an enormous tax burden, while people of non-agricultural professions would be completely free from taxes.

The second part of Liang Ch'i-ch'ao's essay was an attempt to criticize land nationalization from the economic viewpoint. First, he criticized Henry George's theory that land was created by no man and that its benefits should be monopolized by nobody. If this were true, it could be said that everything was a product of society and nothing should be privately owned. Liang's argument was based on chapter 6 of Kōtō sozei genron (Theory on Advanced Taxes)

45

by Tanaka Hozumi (1876-1944), who in turn based his arguments on a European scholar. Liang maintained that land ownership was a kind of private ownership and had been recognized by society as a justified right. Denial of private ownership of land contradicted the recognition of private ownership in general. Liang quoted Kawakami Hajime (1879-1946), who said that economic activities were motivated by men's desire to own things privately. Private ownership provided incentive for economic progress, through which the people's wealth and hence the national wealth increased. If private ownership was abolished, would people still work hard and would the economy be affected as a consequence? Liang expressed his disagreement with Richard Ely's contention that private ownership was based on plunder. Moreover, in China the small landowner-cultivator made up the vast majority of the agricultural population, and most landowners obtained their land through hard work and thrift. To deprive them of this land was tantamount to depriving them of their hard-earned fruits and of the incentive for diligence. The Min-pao promised to compensate the original landowners for the loss of land to the government. But where could the new government find the funds for this redemption payment? Liang held that land should be classified into four categories: city-land (i-ti), country-fields (yeh-ti), ownerless-land (tzu-yu-ti), and owned-land (yu-chu-ti). City-land could be state or municipally owned

and ownerless land should be nationalized;
but the state should not intrude into
country fields belonging to private own-
ers. Furthermore, a piece of land cultivated by many small farmers might yield
less than when cultivated by fewer larger
farmers employing new agricultural tech-
niques, which tillers of smaller means
could not afford. In sum, Liang charged
that the T'ung-meng Hui's land program
was a "suicidal policy" for China. He
was equally critical of the Min-pao's
plan to prevent the rise of large Chinese
capitalists. He quoted the German economist Gustav Schmoller (1838-1917) as having said that the industrialists played a
most important role in the national economy. With making profits as the goal,
the industrialists frequently risked new
experiments and innovations designed to
adjust production to the needs of consumption and thereby promoted the well-being
of the people. Public enterprise was in
many cases plagued by inefficiency and
conservatism because the main concern of
government officials was merely to fulfill
their administrative tasks, not to make
innovations. Moreover, even in the rela-
tively sound British polity, public enterprise had engendered the growth of the
corruption and tyranny of bureaucracy.
The educational level of the Chinese people was far below that of the English, and
the future new government initially would
not be able to establish a full range of
laws right away. Under such circumstances,
to entrust all important production enter-

prises to government officials would en-
hance the power of officialdom and lead
to the disastrous appearance of a "democratic dictatorship" (min-chu chuan-cheng)
of power concentrated in the hands of a
few.

The third part of Liang Ch'i-ch'ao's
essay was an attempt to criticize land
nationalization with regard to the issue
of whether it would be able to solve the
so-called social problem, namely the gap
between the rich and the poor. He first
set forth his interpretation of the goals
of socialist doctrine, which, according to
him, were two-fold: (1) to remedy the ills
of the monopoly of capital by large capitalists so as to protect small capitalists; (2) to harmonize the conflicts of
interest between the capitalists and the
proletarians so as to protect the proletarians. When considering social problems,
Liang argued, not only the poor but also
the rich should be taken into account, for
society should be monopolized neither by
the rich nor by the poor. The reason
European and American socialists paid more
attention to the poor was that the rich had
long enjoyed special privileges. Liang
felt nationalization of all production organization might lead to the achievement of
the goal of equal distribution of wealth
but was impractical. Even if it were
carried out, it would not be economically
beneficial to the people. On the other
hand, social reform measures would be able
to realize this goal without nationalizing
the land. As to the land nationalization

program of the <u>Min-pao</u>, it would never be able to achieve the goal of equalizing wealth.

Liang Ch'i-ch'ao devoted the remainder of his article to proving the above points. He said that many of the richest were not landowners, but were industrial manufacturers and business men who made their fortunes through non-agricultural investments and had to pay little, if any, land tax. It was possible to become rich more easily and quickly through non-agricultural investments, for example, stocks. Therefore, any change in the land system would not greatly affect the richest. While land nationalization could not check the tyranny of the rich, it would cause the poor small landowner-cultivators to shoulder an enormous tax and hence create great misery for them. Moreover, there was one fundamental problem, to which the <u>Min-pao</u> offered no solution. China lacked sufficient arable land for her agricultural population. Even if the state nationalized all land, only half of China's population would have a share of land to till. With the general tendency of population increase, the problem of insufficency of arable land would become even more acute in the future and might cause another revolution in a few decades.

As indicated at the end of the third installment, "A Further Refutation of a Certain Paper's Land Nationalization Doctrine" was not completed. However,

what was intended to be the remainder of
the article never appeared. In fact,
Liang did not write further criticism of
the Min-pao's social program, and shortly
afterward the Hsin-min ts'ung-pao sus-
pended publication. The last issue of
the journal, number 96, was dated 20 November 1907.


Wu Chung-yao

It is appropriate to mention here an article entitled "She-hui chu-i lun" (A Discussion of Socialism) appearing in the
89th issue of the Hsin-min ts'ung-pao.[56]
The author, Wu Chung-yao, was a close follower of Liang Ch'i-ch'ao,[57] and this article was related to Liang's polemic with
the Min-pao group. Liang wrote in his
preface to Wu's article that socialism occupied a most important position in the
contemporary world. The importance of socialism in a given country was in proportion to the increase of the national
wealth. In Liang's opinion, China had no
room for the rise of socialism, as she was
industrially underdeveloped. However, the
Chinese people should have a knowledge of
socialism as a part of the world's problems. Casting his eyes in the direction
of the Min-pao writers, Liang charged that
those "wildly ambitious men often talk
about socialism intending to utilize it as
a tool of agitation. They have no understanding whatsoever of its real nature, not
having studied it. This only increases the

50

people's bewilderment." He also said that
his articles refuting the Min-pao group
dealt with the question of whether socialism suited China but were not studies of
socialism, while Wu's work, the result of
extensive research, would balance this de-
ficiency. The bibliography of Wu's article shows that the works consulted were
all in Chinese and Japanese.

Wu Chung-yao's article was intended to
consist of eight chapters, but for unknown reasons, only three chapters were
ever published. The first chapter discussed the origins of the word socialism
and categories of divisions of socialism.
It divided socialism into two main categories: the "narrow" and the "broad."
"Narrow socialism aimed to destroy the
existing social structure and reconstruct
it anew. It is also called revolutionary
socialism." "Broad socialism aimed to
rectify, within the existing social
structure, the shortcomings of individualism. It is also called social reformism." According to Wu, although there
were many brands of socialism, they all
aimed to remedy social ills, differing
only in means to achieve the same goal.
Their means could be divided into two
kinds: one was to relieve the distress
of both the rich and poor classes, and
the other of only the poor class. Wu
himself was in favor of broad socialism,
which in his opinion was needed in China,
but narrow socialism "definitely should
not be practiced" there. His essay was
intended to vindicate this view.

51

Wu Chung-yao asserted that communism and anarchism appeared to be similar to narrow socialism but actually were different. The goal of communism was to abolish all private property, whereas socialism aimed only at the abolition of private lands and capital. The goal of anarchism was to abolish government so that the individual could act according to his free will, but socialism advocated that the state should have control over industrial activities.

The second chapter of Wu Chung-yao's essay gave five reasons for the rise of socialism: (1) the economic gap between the rich and the poor caused by the industrial revolution; (2) the inability of former slaves to become economically independent following their political emancipation; (3) the fraudulent practices of the rich tolerated by the laissez-faire legal system after the abolition of feudalism; (4) the spread of economic laissez-faire theories and machinery; and (5) the decline of philanthropic works resulting from the ascendency of atheism. In Wu's judgment, these five factors explained the reason why socialism arose in order to meet the needs of the time.

In the third chapter Wu Chung-yao asserted that the goal of narrow socialism was public ownership of the important elements of the means of production, namely land and capital. This goal differed from public ownership of such unimportant elements of the means of production as roads, canals, postal and telegraph service, railways, mines, and forests, which was practiced in many contemporary countries. Narrow socialism held that the people should work according to their abilities and that production was for the purpose of consumption but not of commerce.

## Feng Tzu-yu

Apart from Chu Chih-hsin and Hu Han-min, Feng Tzu-yu (1880-1958) was another strong advocate of land nationalization and critic of Liang Ch'i-ch'ao. Feng's article, "Min-sheng chu-i yü Chung-kuo cheng-chih ke-ming chih ch'ien-t'u" (The Min-sheng Principle and the Future of the Chinese Political Revolution), which appeared in the fourth issue of the Min-pao,[58] was the first essay of the journal devoted to a discussion of the min-sheng principle. Like Chu Chih-hsin, Feng flatly identified min-sheng chu-i with the Japanese term shakai shugi. They also shared the view that the rise of socialism was shown by the growing strength of socialist parties in parliaments, and particularly by the fact that members of the Social Democratic Party occupied half of the seats in Germany's national parliament. Feng noted that "at present all of Germany's domestic policies are based on socialism, and the growth rate of its industries and commerce tends to surpass those of England and the United States." Socialist parties in England and France had also made great leaps in the general elections, but the striking event was the Russian Revolution

53

of 1905, which Feng attributed to the work of "the Russian Socialist Party" and which in his opinion might serve as a guide for China's future course. American capitalists with the system of trusts had oppressed the workers and attempted to exclude Chinese labor; however, American workers reacted with general strikes--clear evidence of the growth of min-sheng chu-i in the New World. The torrents of socialism were so powerful that they had even advanced as far as East Asia. Although the Japanese Socialist Party led by Kōtoku Shūsui and Katayama Sen was still in its infancy and suppressed by the government, state socialism was practiced in Japan, as shown by the fact that railways, tobacco, wine, sugar, and other industries were government monopolies. Thus, Feng argued that the above events illustrated the global influence of socialism, which would have a bearing on the future of the Chinese political revolution.

Like many of his contemporaries, Feng Tzu-yu understood the goal of socialism as bridging the gap between the rich and the poor and promoting the well-being of the majority. Industrialization had made London a place of sharp contrast between sumptuousness and slums. In America, trusts had smothered most of the middle class, leaving only the large capitalists and workers. Capitalists were so powerful in the United States that they even controlled presidential elections. Therefore, trusts were targets of socialism. And yet, Liang Ch'i-ch'ao wanted to introduce monstrous trusts into China, charged Feng. It was said that socialism would destroy all incentive for competition and bring regression in the world. Such a view was outdated, in Feng's opinion. Man's concern for public welfare and his sense of honor increased in proportion to the development of civilization. Feng reported that he had encountered, in his extracurricular readings as well as in school textbooks, criticisms of socialism. According to him, those who disapproved of socialism did so because they felt that social ills in Europe and America were too deep-rooted to be rectified and that any forced rectification would lead to great disaster. However, these fears were unfounded. Of all socialist schools, Feng paid special homage to the German.

Despite his criticism of Liang Ch'i-ch'ao, Feng Tzu-yu actually shared with Liang the view that socialist ideas existed in ancient China, for example, in the well-field system. Feng added, however, that the well-field system implied the principle of socialism, although it was not an embodiment of socialism. Like Liang, Feng considered the land reforms of Wang Mang and Wang An-shih to have been based on socialist precepts. Feng regarded the public granaries system of the Taipings as another example of Chinese socialism. If China would apply its lost socialist tradition to the newly discovered principles of Europe and America, it might become more advanced than the West. Yet ignorant Chinese scholars such as Liang Ch'i-ch'ao held that socialism was not suitable for China. Liang had even forgotten that around 1899 he himself had advocated the inevitability of a world economic revolution as well as a feminist revolution.

Having assumed that socialism was needed in China, Feng Tzu-yu discussed the timing for carrying it out. It should be carried out at the very outset of the political revolution by the military government. This would be a golden opportunity to curb the growth of the Chinese capitalists, who were still limited in wealth and in numbers. At present, China was the only country in the entire world that had not been affected by the ills of capitalism. It could become a socialist model for other nations to follow.

According to Feng Tzu-yu, state socialism was most suitable for the era of military government, and the basic principle of state socialism was equalization of land rights as advocated by Henry George. Feng said that in ancient times there was no such thing as land rent, and even during the middle ages land rent had increased very slowly. Only in the nineteenth century did large landowners emerge. Thereafter land rents increased greatly, causing the majority of the poor to live like a slave class. Land nationalization, namely equalization of land rights, was

56

the only way to remedy this situation.
It consisted of nationalization of forests,
mines, communications, and farming-land
in cities. The British had been adopting
land nationalization with great effective-
ness in Australia and making it a socialist paradise. To implement land nationalization in China would be easier than
in other countries because in the past
most of the forests, mines, and roads had
been government owned and there had been
a large amount of official land.

Feng Tzu-yu noted that various socialist parties generally agreed on the issue
of land nationalization, but disagreement
over methods of taxation had led to
divisions into separate parties. He saw
the single tax as the most suitable method
for China and the easiest one, because
China had practiced the Single Whip
System for more than two hundred years
since Emperor K'ang-hsi ordered the
merging of corvée labor with the land tax.
There was no great difference in principle
between Henry George's Single Tax and the
Manchus' Single Whip. The difference was
that the latter was designed by the
Manchus to control the Han people and
consequently had bad results. Moreover,
in recent years the Manchus had imposed
various surtaxes on the people and in fact
discarded the Single Whip system. Nevertheless, this past experience might serve
as an aid to the new republican government
in making reforms, and it would make it
easier for China to practice the Single
Tax.

57

In Feng's opinion, the Single Tax had many merits: mitigation of the inequality between the rich and the poor, increase in productivity, simplification of taxation methods, and assurance of ample revenues. Once land nationalization was practiced in China, its land tax would be comparable to that of all Europe. Using this income, political and social reforms could be undertaken overnight, and the power of Europe and America would then lag behind China. This bright prospect made Feng conclude his essay by urging his party to study socialism, land nationalization doctrine, and Single Tax doctrine, and to adopt these as the administrative principles of the future new government.

Before discussing other Min-pao articles pertaining to socialism, it is appropriate to consider where Feng Tzu-yu may have obtained his knowledge about socialism. He was born in Japan, where his father, from Nan-hai, Kwangtung, was in the stationery and printing business. In 1896 the Feng family helped Sun Yat-sen found a branch of the Hsing-Chung Hui in Yokohama, and Tzu-yu, then 14 years old, became its youngest member. In 1900, Feng enrolled in Waseda University and became deeply involved in the Chinese students' anti-Manchu activities. In 1903 he was appointed the Tokyo correspondent of the Chung-kuo jih-pao (China Daily) of Hong Kong, the organ of the Hsing-Chung Hui. Having joined the T'ung-meng Hui, in late 1905 he went to Hong Kong to take charge of the T'ung-meng Hui's branch there and

of the Chung-kuo jih-pao.[59] The article
"The Min-sheng Principle and the Future
of the Chinese Political Revolution" was
first published in the Chung-kuo jih-pao
and reprinted with revisions in the Min-
pao. The above brief account of Feng's
life up to the time he wrote the said
essay suggests that his knowledge of socialism came from Japanese sources.

Sung Chiao-jen

Sung Chiao-jen (1882-1913) and Liao Chung-
k'ai (1878-1925), two other principal
figures of the T'ung-meng Hui, also took
part in introducing socialist ideas. Sung
translated, with minor alterations of his
own, an article by Ōsugi Sakae in the
first issue of the journal Shakai shugi
kenkyū (Studies in Socialism, founded by
Sakai Toshihiko in early 1906) and published it under his pen name Ch'iang-chai
in the fifth issue of the Min-pao as "Wan-
kuo she-hui-tang ta-hui shih-lüeh" (Brief
History of the Socialist International).
This article gives a general account of
the Second International from 1877 to
1904. The introduction has a ring of
radicalism. It states that the world's
population could be divided into two
classes: the class which plunders and the
class which is plundered, namely the bourgeoisie (fu-shen) and the proletariat
(p'ing-min). The former monopolized the
means of production and enslaved the latter, which provided labor. The division
into capital and labor created the problem
of wages. The inequality between the two
classes was extreme, with one in heaven
and the other in hell. If this was not

59

done away with, the entire human race
would become "straw dogs" (ch'u-kou, literally meaning something worthless, thrown
away after being used in magical rites).
Yet the proletariat was not powerless; it
had awakened and made a declaration of war
against the bourgeoisie through the voice
of Proudhon, saying that property was
theft. Thus the class struggle (chieh-chi
tou-cheng) had already begun, and the vic-
tory would definitely belong to the majority proletariat. Here Sun quoted the Communist Manifesto: "The Communists disdain
to conceal their views and aims. They
openly declare that their ends can be at-
tained only by the forcible overthrow of
all social conditions. Let the ruling
classes tremble at a Communist revolution.
The proletarians have nothing to lose but
their chains. They have a world to win.
Workingmen of all countries, unite!"

Liao Chung-k'ai

Liao Chung-k'ai published in the seventh
issue of the Min-pao,[61] under the pen name
Yüan-shih, a translation of a chapter of
A Handbook of Socialism by William Dwight
Porter Bliss (1856-1926), an American Christian socialist and the author of several
books on socialism. Entitled "She-hui chu-
i ta-kang" (Outline History of Socialism),
the article maintained that although socialist ideals could be traced to ancient
primitive societies, the socialist move-

ment in modern times started with the year
1817, when Robert Owen proposed to the
parliament a social-communal program,
Saint Simon established his socialism, and
Felicite Lamennais (1782-1854) published
the earliest Christian socialist doctrine.
It provided a sketchy account of this movement from 1817 to 1880, from Owen through
Lassalle, Bakunin, Marx, and Engels.
Born and raised in the United States until
17 sui, Liao was fluent in English in addition to Chinese and Japanese. However,
it is unknown whether Liao's translation
was based on an English version or a Japanese one that may have existed at the time.


Yeh Hsia-sheng


Yeh Hsia-sheng, a lesser figure of the
T'ung-meng Hui compared to the other men
mentioned above, published under the pen
name Meng-tieh-sheng in the seventh issue
of Min-pao an article called "Wu-cheng-
fu-tang yü ke-ming-tang chih shuo-ming"
(An Explanation of the Anarchist Parties
and Revolutionary Parties). It was intended to distinguish anarchism from
political revolution and social revolution. According to Yeh, anarchism denied
the necessity of government or the existence of laws and aimed to attain freedom
and equality through destructive means.
Anarchist activities could not be regarded as revolutionary activities, because
they caused only destruction, not construction. Anarchism wanted no govern-

61

ment, whereas political revolution aimed to consolidate the state. Anarchism wanted to destroy government of whatever form, regardless of dictatorship or constitutionalism; political revolution destroyed only dictatorship but attempted to establish constitutionalism. Anarchism despised laws; political revolution looked forward to the creation of good laws.

For Yeh Hsia-sheng the goal of the social revolution was socialism. In his opinion, socialism originated from the French revolution. Until the mid-19th century it was in fact identical with anarchism since both practiced destructive means. "Peaceful socialism" prevailed in Europe only after 1864 following the establishment of the International Workingmen's Association in London with Marx (Ma-erh-k'e) as the leader. Thereafter, the proletariat tried to unite. However, due to differences in economic and industrial development, workers' organizations varied in different countries; for example, England had labor unions (lao-tung tsu-ho, rōdō kumiai) and Germany practiced socialism, leading to the separation of socialism from anarchism in 1883. Henceforth, socialism has as its goal to harmonize (t'iao-ho) the individual's interests with the general interests of society, striving for harmony between individual and society. For the purpose of equalizing properties, socialism had to give power to the state and to utilize government. However, the kind of government utilized by socialism

62

should be a republican polity, because equality existed only in republics. To demonstrate that socialism was no utopia but prescribed concrete measures to be taken, the author quoted, for the second time in the Chinese language, the ten-point program in the Communist Manifesto. Except for a few words, his translation was identical with that by Chu Chih-hsin in the "Short Biographies of German Social Revolutionaries."

Yeh Hsia-sheng thought that socialism differed from anarchism in three ways. First, anarchism aimed to destroy government, while socialism wanted to utilize government. Second, anarchism had no regard for laws, while socialism followed laws and good government. Third, the undertakings of anarchism were for absolute individualism, while socialist enterprise was peaceful, orderly, and compatible with the principle of fraternity. However, these were differences in means. The ultimate goal of the two doctrines was the same--complete freedom of the individual. Nevertheless, Yeh was for socialism because he felt that men had to live in groups.

In addition to what has been mentioned above, there are two more articles in the Min-pao worthy of mention. These were translations of works by Miyasaki Tamizō, a Japanese advocate of land nationalization. In one, "T'u-ti fu-ch'üan t'ung-chih-hui chu-i-shu" (Program of the Society for the Restoration of Land

63

Rights),[62] Miyasaki maintained that men
were born with equal rights to the use of
land and that the Society aimed to restore
these natural rights to all.  The other,
entitled "Ou-Mei she-hui ke-ming yün-tung
chih chung-lei chi p'ing-lun" (A Classifi-
cation and Commentary on Social Revolutionary Movements in Europe and America),[63] was
written under Miyasaki's pen name Junkō.
It classified contemporary socialist movements into three categories:  (1) the socialism of Marx and Engels, who advocated
the abolition of private ownership of land
and capital; (2) anarchism of three types:
philosophical anarchism for individual
freedom, Christian anarchism for brother-
hood, and the destructive anarchism of
Bakunin advocating the destruction of existing social structures; (3) the theory
of the equality of land, which consisted
of two schools led by Henry George and
Alfred Wallace respectively.


Summary of the Controversy

Having discussed at considerable length
the controversy over socialism between the
Min-pao and the Hsin-min ts'ung-pao during
the years 1905-1907, it is well to reca-
pitulate some of the important facts pre-
sented above.

Whatever the depth of their understanding of Western socialism, the Min-pao
writers shared a common trait with the
Western socialists in their advocacy of

64

economic quality for the majority. In this sense they can be considered, as they claimed, to be within the socialist currents of thought of their times. However, they differed from their Western counterparts in another respect. To most Western socialists, socialism was a cure for capitalist ills, whereas to Sun Yat-sen and his followers it was a preventive. Faced with the reality that China lagged far behind the West in wealth and power, the Chinese socialists, regardless of differences in shades of opinion, tended to agree that capitalism had not arrived in China. However, the existence of private ownership of property was a salient fact of China's economic life, and even though the gap between the rich and the poor in China was not as great as that in the advanced West, there had been a tendency for land to come under the control of a minority of landowners, who exploited the majority peasant-cultivators. In the eyes of the Min-pao writers, land was the most important production factor. With industrialization the landowners would inevitably become landowner-capitalists possessing two means of production, leaving only the third, labor, to the peasant-proletarian. The most effective methods to prevent this undesirable possibility were nationalization of land and of large industries and appropriation of unearned increase in land values, measures which constituted the main contents of the social revolution as envisioned by the T'ung-meng Hui. The state would become the sole and largest capitalist-landowner of the country, promoting the well-being of the people and undertaking large-scale social-economic reforms, which would enable China to outstrip the formerly advanced West. Not only could China thus bypass the capitalist age and the ills accompanying it, by virtue of this direct and painless transformation from backwardness to socialism it would become a model for other nations to follow. The Min-pao group believed that it would not be difficult to implement these policies at the very outset of the political revolution. For, in addition to the fact that capitalism had not taken root on Chinese soil, the principle of economic equality was not foreign to the Chinese heritage.

It might be said that the Min-pao socialists viewed China's poverty with a sense of national pride. In their vision of a viable future, they transformed it into an asset rather than a handicap for national salvation. Perhaps they should be regarded as revolutionary visionaries, whose outlook was tinged with impatience and optimism. This attitude of the Chinese pioneers searching for a short cut to a socialist ideal is reminiscent in some ways of that of many radicals of the May 4th generation. Their exaggeration of the social-economic ills of the West and their confidence in building China into a socialist model may not sound unfamiliar to students of contemporary China. Their aspirations seem to have anticipat-

ed a current of the intellectual-political
history of twentieth century China.

If the Min-pao socialists could be tak-
en as forerunners of a type of latter-day
men of action working for a more direct
and faster road to a socialist China, Liang
Ch'i-ch'ao might be regarded as a repre-
sentative of another type of Chinese intellectual advocating a gradual and evolutionary process toward national wealth.
Actually, both parties had the enrichment
of the nation as their economic goal. The
question was, how? Contrary to the Min-
pao concept of nipping capitalism and its
accompanying ills in the bud, Liang saw
the growth of Chinese capital as essential
to the expansion of the national economy.
If the West had to undergo the stage of
capitalism, was it possible for China to
bypass it? The problem of production appeared to him more urgent in China than
the problem of distribution. Even at the
expense of the interests of the proletariat, the government should protect, instead of curbing, Chinese capitalists in
order to enable them to withstand the economic infiltration of foreign powers. Socialism represented "beautiful and lofty"
ideas ("Miscellaneous Answers to a Certain
Journal"), but it could not yet be carried
out in China since it had not been realized even in the advanced West.

Reviewing this historical controversy,
it is difficult not to notice the absence
of a reference to the Russian Marxists in

both the Min-pao and the Hsin-min ts'ung-
pao. Some have argued that the Russian
revolution of 1905 provided an incentive
for the T'ung-meng Hui's advocacy of si-
multaneous political and social revolutions in China.[64] True, both Chu Chih-
hsin and Feng Tzu-yu described, in early
1906, the Russian revolution as a social
revolution. However, this is no proof at
all that the Russians brought Marxism to
the Chinese. In fact, there is no evidence to show that the Min-pao group had
any knowledge of Russian Marxism. Even
the Communist historian Li Shu had to
admit: "They had not the slightest idea
about the struggle between the two factions of the Russian Social Democratic
Party--the Bolsheviks and the Mensheviks.
They indiscriminately called all Russian
political parties of different classes as
the 'people's party'--min-tang, the same
title which they had assigned to themselves."[65] On the other hand, the Min-
pao seemed to have a fascination with
Russian populism or anarchism, on which
it published several articles, all of
which were translations from Japanese
works.[66]

# 3. MODERN CHINESE TERMS OF JAPANESE ORIGIN

Apart from the above facts, linguistic evidence alone seems to indicate that the Japanese played the key role in introducing socialism to China. Almost all the essential Chinese terms used in the documents under survey came from the Japanese.

A set of Chinese terms, selected from the literature analyzed, is given below. These terms may not necessarily be Marxian, but they are essential in discussions of socialist ideas. They are only selected examples; there are many others that we cannot include here. The origins of these terms have been traced by consulting monographs on the modern Chinese language. The most useful reference has been Kao Ming-k'ai and Liu Cheng-tan, Hsien-tai Han-yü wai-lai tz'u yen-chiu (A Study of Terms of Foreign Origin in the Modern Chinese Language) (Peking: Wen-tzu kai-ke ch'u-pan she, 1958).[67]

A few words must be said concerning the criterion used in classifying these terms. As is well known, the Japanese language consists of two main elements: kanji (Chinese characters) and kana (Japanese syllabaries). Translations and transliterations of foreign words use either kanji or kana. The list below includes only Japanese kanji terms. We

69

have followed A Study of Terms of Foreign Origin in the Modern Chinese Language in classifying Chinese terms of Japanese origin into three categories. First, compounds made of kanji that are found in pre-modern Japanese and do not appear in classical Chinese; for example, the term yōso for "element" (yao-su). Second, terms that existed in classical Chinese but were utilized by the Japanese to translate Western words with meanings that frequently differed, sometimes considerably, from the original classical Chinese. For example, the compound ke-ming first appeared in the Book of Changes, meaning to alter the Mandate (of Heaven). The Japanese adopted this classical Chinese expression to denote "revolution," and then the modern Chinese followed suit. Third, compounds which did not exist in classical Chinese and were invented by the Japanese to translate, and in some cases to transliterate, Western terms. To take another instance, there was no such compound as wu-chih in classical Chinese, although each character existed in classical Chinese as separate words. The Japanese first combined the two kanji, wu and chih, to denote "matter" or "substance."


Terms Found in Pre-Modern Japanese

|  | Chinese | Japanese |
|---|---|---|
| chan-k'ai | 展開 | tenkai |
| (unfolding, development, evolution) | | |

70

| | | |
|---|---|---|
| ch'ang-ho (occasion, case) | 場合 | baai |
| cheng-chuang (symptoms) | 症狀 | shōjō |
| chi-t'uan (group, collective body) | 集團 | shūdan |
| chieh-chüeh (solution, settlement) | 解決 | kaiketsu |
| chiao-huan (exchange, interchange) | 交換 | kōkan |
| chiao-t'ung (traffic, communication) | 交通 | kōtsū |
| chieh-chin (contiguity, proximity) | 接近 | sekkin |
| chieh-yüeh (economy, frugality, saving) | 節約 | setsuyaku |
| chih-hsing (execution, performance) | 執行 | shikkō |
| chih-p'ei (management, control) | 支配 | shihai |
| ch'in-hai (infringement, trespass) | 侵害 | shingai |
| ching-yen (experience) | 經驗 | keiken |
| ch'ing-ch'iu (demand, request) | 請求 | seikyū |

71

ch'u-hsi 出席 shusseki
(attendance, presence)

ch'u-hsing 處刑 shokei
(punishment, execution)

ch'u-hsü 儲蓄 chochiku
(saving)

ch'u-pu 初步 shoho
(first step, rudiments)

chü-li 距離 kyori
(distance)

ch'ü-ti 取締 torishimari
(control, regulation, supervision)

ch'üan-wei 權威 ken'i
(authority, power)

fang-chen 方針 hōshin
(course, policy, principle)

fu-wu 服務 fukumu
(service)

hsiang-hsiang 想像 sōzō
(imagination, supposition)

k'e-fu 克服 kokufuku
(conquest, subjugation)

ko-pieh 個別 kobetsu
(individual case)

ku-chang 故障 koshō
(hindrance, obstacle)

72

kung-t'ung 共同 kyōdō
    (cooperation, common action)

li-wai 例外 reigai
    (exception)

mu-piao 目標 mokuhyō
    (mark, goal, target)

nei-jung 内容 naiyō
    (content, substance)

pi-yao 必要 hitsuyō
    (necessity, requirement)

piao-hsien 表現 hyōgen
    (expression, manifestation)

pu ching-ch'i 不景氣 fukeiki
    (depression, slackness)

shen-ch'ing 申請 shinsei
    (application, request)

shen-fen 身分 mibun
    (social position)

shih-ch'ang 市場 shijō
    (market) (ichiba)

shou-hsü 手續 tetsuzuki
    (procedure)

t'e-pieh 特別 tokubetsu
    (special)

t'e-shu 特殊 tokushu
    (special, peculiar)

73

t'i-yen　　　　體驗　　　　　taiken
　　(experience)

t'iao-chih　　調製　　　　chōsei
　　(manufacture, preparation)

t'ing-chan　　停戰　　　　teisen
　　(cease fire, armistice)

t'ing-chih　　停止　　　　teishi
　　(suspension, stay)

ts'ang-k'u　　倉庫　　　　sōko
　　(warehouse, storehouse)

tso-chan　　　作戰　　　　sakusen
　　(military operations, maneuvers)

tso-wu　　　　作物　　　　sakumotsu
　　(crops)

tsung-chi　　　總計　　　　sōkei
　　(sum total)

tsung-chiao　　宗教　　　　shūkyō
　　(religion)

yao-su　　　　要素　　　　yōso
　　(element)

yao-tien　　　要點　　　　yōten
　　(main point)

74

# Classical Chinese Expressions First Used by Japanese to Translate Western Terms  (Source Listed with Each Item)

| Chinese | | Japanese |
|---|---|---|
| cheng-chih (government, politics) Shih-ching | 政治 詩經 | seiji |
| chi-chi (positive) Chou i | 積極 周易 | sekkyoku |
| chi-hua (plan, project) Han shu | 計劃 漢書 | keikaku |
| chi-hsieh (machinery) Chuang Tzu | 機械 莊子 | kikai |
| chi-hui (opportunity) Han Yü 韓愈 , Yü Liu Chung-ch'eng shu 與柳中丞書 | 機會 | kikai |
| chi-kuan (machine, organ, means) Huang T'ing-chien shih 黃庭堅詩 | 機關 | kikan |
| chi-lu (record, document) Hou Han-shu | 記錄 後漢書 | kiroku |

chia-she 假設 kasetsu
(hypothetical)
<u>Han shu</u> 漢書

chiao-chi 交際 kōsai
(intercourse, association)
<u>Meng Tzu</u> 孟子

chiao-i 交易 kōeki
(trade, commerce)
<u>I ching</u> 易經

chiao-liu 交流 kōryū
(interchange)
<u>Hsin T'ang shu</u> 新唐書

chiao-she 交涉 kōshō
(negotiation, discussion)
<u>Fan Ch'eng-ta shih</u> 范成大詩

chiao-shou 教授 kyōju
(teaching, professor)
<u>Shih chi</u> 史記

chiao-yü 教育 kyōiku
(education)
<u>Meng Tzu</u> 孟子

chieh-chi 階級 kaikyū
(class)
<u>San kuo chih</u> 三國志

chieh-fang 解放 kaihō
(liberation, release)
<u>Chu Tzu yü-lei</u> 朱子語類

chien-t'ao 檢討 kentō
(examination, study)
official title in Sung and Ming

76

chih-ch'ih　　支持　　　　shiji
　(support)
Po Liang shih　　柏梁詩

chih-shih　　知識　　　chishiki
　(knowledge)
used in Buddhist texts

chin-pu　　進步　　　　shinpo
　(progress)　　　　　　(shimpo)
Ch'uan teng lu　傳燈錄

ching-chi　　經濟　　　keizai
　(economy, economics)
Sung shih　　宋史

ching-li　　經理　　　keiri
　(management, administration)
Shih chi　　史記

chu-hsi　　主席　　　shuseki
　(chief, head)
Shih chi　　史記

chü-t'i　　具體　　　gutai
　(concreteness)
Meng Tzu　　孟子

ch'üan-li　　權利　　　kenri
　(right)
Shih chi　　史記

chüeh-tui　　絕對　　　zettai
　(absolute)
Chin-kang-ching　金剛經

77

chün-shih　軍事　gunji
   (military affairs)
Shih chi　史記

fa-lü　法律　hōritsu
   (law)
Kuan Tzu　管子

fa-tse　法則　hōsoku
   (law, rule)
Shih chi　史記

fang-mien　方面　hōmen
   (direction, side)
Hou Han shu　後漢書

fen-hsi　分析　bunseki
   (analysis)
Han shu　漢書

feng-chien　封建　hōken
   (feudal)
Tso chuan　左傳

fu-ts'ung　服從　fukujū
   (obedience, submission)
Han shu　漢書

hsi-wang　希望　kibō
   (hope, wish, desire)
Han Yü fu shang
   tsai-hsiang shu　韓愈復上宰相書

hsiang-tui　相對　sōtai
   (relativity)
Shih chi　史記

78

hsiao-hua　消化　　　　shōka
　(digestion)
Chou shu　周書

hsien-fa　憲法　　　　kenpō
　(constitution)　　　　(kempō)
Kuo yü Chin-yü　國語晉語

hsin-wen　新聞　　　　shinbun
　(newspaper, press)　　(shimbun)
An te chang-che yen　安得長者言

hsin-yung　信用　　　　shinyō
　(trust, credit)
Tso chuan　左傳

hsing-fa　刑法　　　　keihō
　(criminal law, penal law)
Tso chuan　左傳

huan-ching　環境　　　　kankyō
　(environment, circumstance)
Yüan shih　元史

i-chüeh　議決　　　　giketsu
　(decision, resolution)
Han shu　漢書

i-shu　藝術　　　　geijutsu
　(art)
Hou Han shu　後漢書

i-wei　意味　　　　imi
　(meaning, significance)
Pai Chü-i shih　白居易詩

kai-tsao 改造 kaizō
   (reconstruction)
<u>Tzu-chih t'ung-chien</u> 資治通鑑

k'ang-i 抗議 kōgi
   (protest)
<u>Hou Han shu</u> 後漢書

ke-ming 革命 kakumei
   (revolution)
<u>I ching</u> 易經

k'o-ch'eng 課程 katei
   (course, curriculum)
<u>Shih ching</u> 詩經

kou-tsao 構造 kōzō
   (construction, structure)
<u>Sung shu</u> 宋書

ku-i 故意 koi
   (intention, design)
<u>Tu Fu shih</u> 杜甫詩

k'uai-chi 會計 kaikei
   (account)
<u>Meng Tzu</u> 孟子

kuan-hsi 關係 kankei
   (relation, connection)
<u>Li Wen-chung-kung ch'üan-shu</u> 李文忠公全書

kuei-tse 規則 kisoku
   (rule, regulation)
<u>Li Ch'ün-yü shih</u> 李群玉詩

80

kung-ho　　　共和　　　kyōwa
　(republic)
<u>Shih chi</u>　　史記

kung-chi　　　供給　　　kyōkyū
　(supply, provision)
<u>Tso chuan</u>　　左傳

lao-tung　　　勞働/動　　rōdō
　(labor)
<u>Pai Chü-i shih</u>　白居易詩

li-shih　　　　歷史　　　rekishi
　(history)
<u>Nan Ch'i shu</u>　南齊書

liu-hsing　　　流行　　　ryūkō
　(fashion, vogue)
<u>Meng Tzu</u>　　孟子

lun-li　　　　倫理　　　rinri
　(ethics)
<u>Mao shih cheng-i</u>　毛詩正義

min-chu　　　　民主　　　minshu
　(democracy)
<u>Shu-ching</u>　　書經
　<u>Hai-k'e jih t'an</u>　海客日譚

ming-ling　　　命令　　　meirei
　(order, directive)
<u>Wang Chou shih</u>　王周詩

pao-chang　　　保障　　　hoshō
　(guarantee, security)
<u>Tso chuan</u>　　左傳

pao-hsien 保險 hoken
   (insurance)
<u>Sui shu</u> 隋書

piao-hsiang 表象 hyōshō
   (presentation, symbol)
<u>Hou Han shu</u> 後漢書

p'o-ch'an 破產 hasan
   (bankruptcy)
<u>Hsin T'ang shu</u> 新唐書

she-hui 社會 shakai
   (society)
<u>Tung-ching meng-hua lu</u> 東京夢華錄

sheng-ch'an 生產 seisan
   (production)
<u>Shih chi</u> 史記

shih-yen 試驗 shiken
   (experiment)
<u>Liu Ying shih</u> 劉迎詩

shou-tuan 手段 shudan
   (means)
<u>Hsieh Shang-ts'ai</u>
   <u>yü-lu</u> 謝上蔡語錄

ssu-hsiang 思想 shisō
   (thought, idea)
<u>Ts'ao Chih shih</u> 曹植詩

Su-she 宿舍 shukusha
   (lodging, dormitory)
<u>Shih chi</u> 史記

suan-shu 算術 sanjutsu
(arithmetic)
Han shu 漢書

ti-chu 地主 jinushi
(landlord)
Tso chuan 左傳

t'ieh-tao 鐵道 tetsudō
(railway)
Hang-hai shu-ch'i 航海述奇
    by Chang Te-ming 張德明

t'ou-chi 投機 tōki
(speculation, venture)
T'ang shu 唐書

tsa-chih 雜誌 zasshi
(magazine, journal)
Tu-shu tsa-chih 讀書雜誌

ts'ai-liao 材料 zairyō
(material, data)
Sung shih 宋史

tso-yung 作用 sayō
(action, operation)
T'ien-kung k'ai-wu 天工開物

tsu-chih 組織 soshiki
(organization)
Liao shih 遼史

tzu-jan 自然 shizen
(nature)
Lao Tzu 老子

| | | |
|---|---|---|
| tzu-yu | 自由 | jiyū |
| (liberty, freedom) | | |
| <u>Tu Fu Shih</u> | 杜甫 詩 | |
| | | |
| wei-i | 惟/唯一 | yuiitsu |
| <u>Shu ching</u> | 書經 | |
| | | |
| wen-fa | 文法 | bunpō |
| (grammar) | | (bumpō) |
| <u>Shih chi</u> | 史記 | |
| | | |
| wen-hsüeh | 文學 | bungaku |
| (literature) | | |
| <u>Lun yü</u> | 論語 | |
| | | |
| wen-hua | 文化 | bunka |
| (culture) | | |
| <u>Shuo wan</u> | 說苑 | |
| | | |
| wen-ming | 文明 | bunmei |
| (civilization) | | (bummei) |
| <u>I ching</u> | 易經 | |
| | | |
| yün-tung | 運動 | undō |
| (movement, motion) | | |
| <u>Yü pao tui</u> | 雨雹對 | |
| by Tung Chung-shu | | 董仲舒 |
| | | |
| yü-suan | 預算 | yosan |
| (budget) | | |
| <u>Yeh-lü ch'u-ts'ai shih</u> | 耶律楚材 詩 | |

84

# Kanji Terms Created by Modern Japanese
## (Origins Listed in Parentheses)

| | | |
|---|---|---|
| chai-ch'üan (credit) | 債權 | saiken |
| chai-wu (debt) | 債務 | saimu |
| chan-wang (view, prospect) | 展望 | tenbō (tembō) |
| ch'ang-shih (common sense) | 常識 | jōshiki |
| che-hsüeh (philosophy) | 哲學 | tetsugaku |
| cheng-ts'e (policy) | 政策 | seisaku |
| cheng-fu (government) | 政府 | seifu |
| cheng-tang (political party) | 政黨 | seitō |
| ch'eng-fen (ingredient, component) | 成分 | seibun |
| ch'eng-jen (recognition, admission) | 承認 | shōnin |

chi-chung 集中 shūchū
　(concentration)

chi-ho 集合 shūgō
　(meeting, gathering)

chi-shih 技師 gishi
　(engineer, technician)

ch'i-yeh 企業 kigyō
　(enterprise)

chia-ting 假定 katei
　(assumption, supposition)

chiang-yen 講演 kōen
　(lecture, address)

chieh-fang 借方 karikata
　(debtor)

chieh-lun 結論 ketsuron
　(conclusion)

chien-ting 鑑定 kantei
　(judgement)

ch'ien-t'i 前提 zentei
　(premise)

chih-p'ei li 支配力 shihairyoku
　(controlling power)

chih-ts'ai 制裁 seisai
　(restraint, punishment)

chih-wai fa-ch'üan 治外法權 chigaihōken
　(extraterritoriality)

chih-yüan 職員 shokuin
(staff, personnel)

chih-yüeh 制約 seiyaku
(to condition, control)

chin-chan 進展 shinten
(development, progress)

chin-hua 進化 shinka
(evolution)

chin-k'u 金庫 kinko
(safe)

chin-o 金額 kingaku
(sum, amount of money)

ch'in-fan 侵犯 shinhan
(to violate) (shimpan)

ch'in-lüeh 侵略 shinryaku
(aggression, raid)

ch'in-shih 侵蝕 shinshoku
(erosion, encroachment)

ching-chi hsüeh 經濟學 keizaigaku
(economics)

ching-chi k'ung-huang keizai kyōkō
(economic panic) 經濟恐慌

ching-t'ai 靜態 seitai
(static, stationary)

ch'ing kung-yeh 輕工業 keikōgyō
(light industry)

ch'ing-yüan 請願 seigan
(petition, application)

chou-ch'i 週期 shūki
(periodic time, period)

ch'ou-hsiang 抽象 chūshō
(abstract)

chu-ch'üan 主權 shuken
(sovereignty)

chu-i 主義 shugi
(doctrine, principle)

chu-kuan 主觀 shukan
(subjectivity)

chu-t'i 主體 shutai
(subject, constituency)

chu-tung 主動 shudō
(leadership, initiative)

ch'u-ch'ao 出超 shutchō
(excess of exports over imports)

ch'u-pan 出版 shuppan
(publication, issue)

chuan-mai 專賣 senbai
(monopoly, monopolization) (sembai)

ch'uan-po 傳播 denpa
(propagation) (dempa)

ch'uan-t'ung 傳統 dentō
(tradition, convention)

chung kung-yeh 重工業 (heavy industry) jūkōgyō

chung-ts'ai 仲裁 (arbitration) chūsai

chü-hsien 局限 (localization, limit) kyokugen

chün-kuo chu-i 軍國主義 (militarism) gunkoku shugi

fa hsüeh 法學 (law, jurisprudence) hōgaku

fa-jen 法人 (juridicial (legal) person) hōjin

fa-k'o 法科 (law department) hōka

fa-ting 法定 (legal, statutory) hōtei

fa-t'ing 法庭 (court) hōtei

fan ke-ming 反革命 (counterrevolution) hankakumei

fan-tui 反對 (opposition) hantai

fan-tung 反動 (reaction, rebound) handō

fan-ying 反映 (reflection) hanei

| | | |
|---|---|---|
| fan-ying<br>(reaction, response) | 反應 | hannō |
| fang-an<br>(plan, program) | 方案 | hōan |
| fang-fa<br>(way, method) | 方法 | hōhō |
| fang-shih<br>(formula, method) | 方式 | hōshiki |
| fen-p'ei<br>(division, distribution) | 分配 | bumpai |
| feng-chien chu-i<br>(feudalism) | 封建主義 | hōken shugi |
| feng-chien she-hui<br>(feudal society) | 封建社會 | hōken shakai |
| fou-chüeh<br>(rejection) | 否決 | hiketsu |
| fou-jen<br>(denial, disapproval | 否認 | hinin |
| fou-ting<br>(denial, negation) | 否定 | hitei |
| fu-yüan<br>(demobilization) | 復員 | fukuin |
| hsi-t'ung<br>(system) | 系統 | keito |
| hsia-i<br>(narrow sense) | 狹義 | kyōgi |

hsiao-chi 消極 shōkyoku
   (negative, negativity)

hsiao-fei 消費 shōhi
   (consumption, spending)

hsiao-fei li 消費力 shōhiryoku
   (consumer buying power)

hsiao-lü 効率 kōritsu
   (efficiency)

hsieh-hui 協會 kyōkai
   (association, society)

hsieh-i 協議 kyōgi
   (conference, deliberation)

hsien-chin 現金 genkin
   (cash, specie)

hsien-hsiang 現象 genshō
   (phenomenon)

hsien-shih 現實 genjitsu
   (reality, actuality)

hsien-shih chu-i 現實主義 genjitsu shugi
   (realism)

hsien-shih hsing 現實性 genjitsusei
   (possibility of being realized)

hsien-tai 現代 gendai
   (modern times)

hsien-tai hua 現代化 gendaika
   (modernization)

| | | |
|---|---|---|
| hsin-hao<br>(signal) | 信號 | shingō |
| hsin-li tso-yung<br>(psychological function) | 心理作用 | shinri sayō |
| hsin-wen chi-che<br>(journalist, reporter) | 新聞記者 | shimbun kisha |
| hsing-cheng<br>(administration) | 行政 | gyōsei |
| hsiu-chan<br>(truce, armistice) | 休戰 | kyūsen |
| hsüan-chan<br>(declaration of war) | 宣戰 | sensen |
| hu-hui<br>(reciprocity) | 互惠 | gokei |
| huo-tung<br>(activity) | 活動 | katsudō |
| i-an<br>(bill, measure) | 議案 | gian |
| i-chih<br>(will, volition) | 意志 | ishi |
| i-hui<br>(parliament) | 議會 | gikai |
| i-shih<br>(consciousness) | 意識 | ishiki |
| i-t'u<br>(intention, purpose) | 意圖 | ito |

92

i-wu 義務 (duty, obligation)  gimu

i-yüan 議員 (member of parliament)  giin

jen-ke 人格 (personality, character)  jinkaku

jen-k'ou wen-t'i 人口問題 (population problem)  jinkō mondai

jen-sheng kuan 人生觀 (view of life)  jinseikan

jen-wei-te 人為的 (artificial)  jin-iteki

jen-wen chu-i 人文主義 (humanism)  jimbun shugi

kai-liang 改良 (improvement, reform)  kairyō

kai-k'uo 概括 (summary)  gaikatsu

kai-lun 概論 (outline)  gairon

kai-nien 概念 (concept)  gainen

kai-suan 概算 (rough estimate)  gaisan

k'e-kuan 客觀 (objectivity)  kakkan (kyakkan)

93

k'e-t'i 客體 kakutai
(object) (kyakutai)

ken-pen ti 根本的 konponteki
(rudimentary, (komponteki)
fundamentally)

k'en-ting 肯定 kōtei
(affirmative)

k'o-hsüeh 科學 kagaku
(science)

k'o-neng hsing 可能性 kanōsei
(possibility)

ku-yüan 僱員 koin
(employee)

kua-t'o cheng-chih 寡頭政治 katōseiji
(oligarchy)

kuan-chih 管制 kansei
(control)

kuan-li 管理 kanri
(management, control)

kuan-nien 觀念 kannen
(idea, sense)

kuan-tien 觀點 kanten
(viewpoint)

kuang-i 廣義 kōgi
(broad sense)

kuei-na 歸納 kinō
(induction)

94

kuei-na fa 歸納法 kinōhō
   (inductive method)

kung-chai 公債 kōsai
   (public debt, public bond)

kung-ch'an chu-i 共產主義 kyōsan shugi
   (communism)

kung-ch'an chu-i 共產主義社會 kyōsan shugi
   she-hui shakai
   (communist society)

kung-cheng jen 公證人 koshōnin
   (notary)

kung-k'ai 公開 kōkai
   (open, public)

kung-yeh 工業 kōgyō
   (industry)

kung-yeh hua 工業化 kōgyōka
   (industrialization)

k'ung-chien 空間 kūkan
   (space, room)

kuo-chi 國際 kokusai
   (international)

kuo-chi kung-fa 國際公法 kokusai kōhō
   (international law)

kuo-chi wen-t'i 國際問題 kokusai mondai
   (international problem)

95

kuo-chia she-hui
 chu-i 國家社會主義 kokka shakai
(state socialism) shugi

kuo-tu 過渡 kato
(transitory)

lang-man chu-i 浪漫主義 rōman shugi
(romanticism)

lao-tung-che 勞働者 rōdōsha
(proletarian)

li-ch'ang 立場 tachiba
(standpoint)

li-hsiang 理想 risō
(ideal)

li-lun 理論 riron
(theory)

li-shih 理事 riji
(director, trustee)

lien-lo 連絡 renraku
(connection)

ling-t'u 領土 ryōdo
(territory, domain)

lo-kuan 樂觀 rakkan
(optimism)

lieh-shih 劣勢 ressei
(inferiority)

96

lun-li hsüeh 論理學 ronrigaku
  (logic)

lun-wen 論文 rombun
  (treatise, essay, dissertation)

mei hsüeh 美學 bigaku
  (aesthetics)

mei-hua 美化 bika
  (beautification)

mei-kan 美感 bikan
  (aesthetic feeling)

mei-shu 美術 bijutsu
  (art)

mien-ch'u 免除 menjo
  (exemption, remission)

min-tsu 民族 minzoku
  (race, people, nation)

min-tsu wen-t'i 民族問題 minzoku
  (nationality problem) mondai

ming-t'i 命題 meidai
  (proposition)

mu-ti 目的 mokuteki
  (aim, object)

mu-ti-wu 目的物 mokutekibutsu
  (object)

nei-tsai 內在 naizai
(immanence, inherence)

nu-li she-hui 奴隸社會 dorei shakai
(slave society)

nung-min 農民 nōmin
(peasant, farmer)

nung-min chieh-chi 農民階級 nōmin kaikyū
(peasant class)

ou-jan 偶然 gūzen
(chance, accident)

ou-jan hsing 偶然性 gūzensei
(accident)

p'an-chüeh 判決 hanketsu
(judgement)

p'an-tuan 判斷 handan
(judgement, inference)

pao-cheng 保證 hoshō
(guarantee, assurance)

pao-kao 報告 hōkoku
(report)

pei-ching 背景 haikei
(background)

pei-kuan 悲觀 hikan
(pessimism, originally used in
Buddhist texts)

| | | |
|---|---|---|
| pei-tung<br>(passive) | 被動 | hidō |
| p'ei-chi<br>(rationing, distribution) | 配給 | haikyū |
| pi-jan hsing<br>(necessity, inevitability) | 必然性 | hitsuzensei |
| p'i-p'an<br>(criticism, comment) | 批判 | hihan |
| p'i-p'ing<br>(criticism, comment) | 批評 | hihyō |
| piao-chüeh<br>(vote, division) | 表決 | hyōketsu |
| piao-yen<br>(show, performance) | 表演 | hyōen |
| p'ien-chien<br>(prejudice) | 偏見 | henken |
| p'o-hai<br>(persecution) | 迫害 | hakugai |
| pu-tung-ch'an<br>(immovables, reality) | 不動產 | fudōsan |
| shang-p'in<br>(goods, merchandise) | 商品 | shōhin |
| shang-yeh<br>(commerce, trade) | 商業 | shōgyō |
| she-chiao te<br>(of social intercourse) | 社交的 | shakōteki |

she-hui chu-i 社會主義 shakai shugi
(socialism)

she-hui hsüeh 社會學 shakai gaku
(sociology)

she-hui wen-t'i 社會問題 shakai mondai
(social problem)

she-t'uan 社團 shadan
(corporation, association)

sheng-ch'an kuan-hsi 生產關係 seisan kankei
(production relationship)

sheng-ch'an li 生產力 seisan ryoku
(productivity, producing capacity)

sheng-ch'an shou-tuan 生產手段 seisan shudan
(means of production)

shih-chi 世紀 seiki
(century)

shih-chieh kuan 世界觀 sekai kan
(world outlook)

shih-chien 時間 jikan
(time, period)

shih-tai 時代 jidai
(period, epoch)

shou kung-yeh 手工業 shukōgyō
(handicraft)

shu hsüeh 數學 sūgaku
(mathematics)

| | | |
|---|---|---|
| shuo-ming (explanation) | 說明 | setsumei |
| so-te shui (income tax) | 所得稅 | shotokuzei |
| so-yu ch'üan (ownership) | 所有權 | shoyūken |
| ssu-ch'ao (trend of thought) | 思潮 | shichō |
| tai-fang (creditor) | 貸方 | kashikata |
| tai-piao (representation) | 代表 | daihyō |
| tai-li (agency) | 代理 | dairi |
| tan-wei (unit) | 單位 | tan'i |
| t'an-p'an (negotiation) | 談判 | danpan (dampan) |
| tao-huo-hsien (fuse) | 導火線 | dōkasen |
| t'e-cheng (characteristic, peculiarity) | 特徵 | tokuchō |
| t'e-ch'üan (privilege, special right) | 特權 | tokken |
| t'e-hsü (special permission) | 特許 | tokkyo |

101

t'e-yüeh 特約 tokuyaku
   (special arrangement, special contract)

teng-chi 登記 tōki
   (registration)

ti-chu chieh-chi 地主階級 jinushi
   (landlord class) kaikyū

ti-kuo chu-i 帝國主義 teikoku
   (imperialism) shugi

t'i-an 提案 teian
   (proposal, proposition)

t'i-kung 提供 teikyō
   (offer, proffer)

t'iao-chien 條件 jōken
   (condition, terms)

t'iao-cheng 調整 chōsei
   (regulation, adjustment)

t'iao-chieh 調節 chōsetsu
   (regulation, adjustment)

tien-hsin 電信 denshin
   (telegraph, cable)

tien-hsing 典型 tenkei
   (type, pattern)

tien-li 電力 denryoku
   (electric power)

tien-pao 電報 denpō
   (telegram) (dempō)

tien-yeh 電業 dengyo
(electrical industry)

ting-i 定義 teigi
(definition)

ting-o 定額 teigaku
(fixed amount, specified amount)

tou-cheng 鬥爭 tōsō
(fight, struggle)

t'o-tang 脱黨 dattō
(secession)

t'ou-p'iao 投票 tōhyō
(voting, polling)

t'ou-tzu 投資 tōshi
(investment)

ts'ai-cheng 財政 zaisei
(finance, financial affairs)

ts'ai-fa 財閥 zaibatsu
(plutocracy)

ts'ai-t'uan 財團 zaidan
(foundation)

ts'ai-wu 財務 zaimu
(financial affairs)

ts'an-k'ao shu 參考書 sankōsho
(reference book)

tsu-ho 組合 kumiai
(association, league, union)

103

| | | |
|---|---|---|
| ts'u-chin (promotion) | 促進 | sokushin |
| tsui-hou t'ung-tieh (ultimatum) | 最後通牒 | saigotsūchō |
| tsui-hui kuo (the most favored nation) | 最惠國 | saikeikoku |
| tsung-ho (synthesis) | 綜合 | sōgō |
| tsung-ho fa (method of synthesis) | 綜合法 | sōgōhō |
| tsung-li (premier) | 總理 | sōri |
| tsung-t'i (whole) | 總體 | sōtai |
| tsung tung-yüan (general mobilization) | 總動員 | sōdōin |
| tu-chan (monopoly) | 獨佔 | dokusen |
| tu-ts'ai (dictatorship) | 獨裁 | dokusai |
| t'u-ti wen-t'i (land problem) | 土地問題 | tochi mondai |
| tuan-ting (decision, judgement) | 斷定 | dantei |
| tui-ch'eng (symmetry) | 對稱 | taishō |

104

| | | |
|---|---|---|
| tui-hsiang<br>(object) | 對象 | taishō |
| tui-pi<br>(contrast, comparison) | 對比 | taihi |
| tui-ying<br>(match) | 對應 | taiō |
| t'ui-hua<br>(degeneration) | 退化 | taika |
| t'ui-lun<br>(reasoning) | 推論 | suiron |
| tung-ch'an<br>(movable estate) | 動產 | dōsan |
| tung-chi<br>(motive, incentive) | 動機 | dōki |
| tung-hsiang<br>(trend, tendency) | 動向 | dōkō |
| tung-i<br>(motion) | 動議 | dōgi |
| tung-t'ai<br>(movement) | 動態 | dōtai |
| tung-yüan<br>(mobilization) | 動員 | dōin |
| t'ung-hua tso-yung<br>(assimilation, metabolism) | 同化作用 | dōka sayō |
| t'ung-meng<br>(alliance, league, union) | 同盟 | dōmei |

105

t'ung-meng pa-kung 同盟罷工 dōmei hikō
   (strike, walkout)

tzu-ch'an chieh-chi 資產階級 shisan kaikyū
   (bourgeoisie)

tzu-chih 自治 jichi
   (autonomy, self-government)

tzu-fa te 自發的 jihatsuteki
   (spontaneous)

tzu-jan k'o-hsüeh 自然科學 shizen kagaku
   (natural science)

tzu-pen 資本 shihon
   (capital, fund)

tzu-pen-chia 資本家 shihonka
   (capitalist)

tzu-pen chu-i 資本主義 shihon shugi
   (capitalism)

tzu-pen chu-i she-hui 資本主義社會 shihonshugi shakai
   (capitalist society)

wai-tsai 外在 gaizai
   (externality)

wu-ch'an chieh-chi 無產階級 musan kaikyū
   (propertyless class)

wu-chih 物質 busshitsu
   (matter, substance)

yao-ch'ung 要衝 yōshō
   (key point, strategic point)

106

yen-i 演繹 eneki
  (deduction)

yen-i fa 演繹法 eneki hō
  (method of deduction)

yu-ch'an chieh-chi 有產階級 yūsan kaikyū
  (propertied class)

yu-shih 優勢 yusei
  (superiority)

yüan-lu 原理 genri
  (principle, theory)

yüan-shih kung-ch'an genshi kyōsan
  she-hui 原始共產社會 shakai
  (primitive communist society)

yüan-su 元素 genso
  (element)

yüan-tse 原則 gensoku
  (principle)

# 5. CONCLUSION

The conclusion that socialism was introduced into China primarily through the
Japanese should come as no surprise at
this point, especially in view of the historical circumstances. In general, the
Chinese were indebted in their Westerniza-
tion to the Japanese, whose role in the
development of Chinese studies of social
and political science is particularly ap-
parent. The early years of this century
witnessed a steady increase of Chinese
students in Japan as a result of a series
of post-Boxer educational reforms adopted
by the Ch'ing government. Apart from geo-
graphical proximity and cultural affinity,
Japan attracted Chinese students because
it offered short-term courses in education
and law, degrees which enabled them to se-
cure posts in teaching or government service upon their return home. By 1906
there were 13,000 to 14,000 Chinese students in Japan, with only a few hundred in
Europe and the United States. Meanwhile,
a large percentage of Chinese books on
Western subjects were translated from the
Japanese,[68] so that linguistic evidence
alone reveals the extent of influence.
The earliest Chinese dictionaries on
Western knowledge contain an enormous
number of Japanese terms.[69] Out of about
1,500 terms of foreign origin found in

modern Chinese, for example, more than half originated in Japan.[70]

The Russian role as China's educator in modern world affairs was by comparison far less significant. Although listed in the T'ung-wen Kuan curriculum, the result of the study of Russian language was negligible. Nor were there many Chinese who studied in Russia during the later Ch'ing and early Republican periods.[71] Although a significant number of Chinese students went to Russia in the 1920s, prior to the Communist take-over the only Chinese school specializing in Russian instruction was the Russian Language Institute in Peking, designed to train professionals for either the Chinese consulates in Russia or the Chinese Eastern Railway. We cannot go into detail here on the history of China's Russian education, which should be the topic of a separate monograph. It suffices to say that until the 1950s not a single competently devised Russian-Chinese dictionary was available [72] and even Communist versions relied on the old Japanese sources.[73]

The foregoing pages also throw light on some characteristics of Chinese Marxism. From the very beginning the Chinese regarded equalization of wealth as the goal of socialism, and this idea remained entrenched in the minds of many Chinese Communists at least as late as the 1920s.[74] The concept of class struggle was not stressed. Some like Liang

109

Ch'i-ch'ao and Yeh Hsia-sheng explicitly emphasized the harmony of class interests as a socialist aim. Throughout the documents under survey the only mention of class struggle is in Chu Chih-hsin's "Short Biographies of German Social Revolutionaries" and "The Progress of the Proletariat in the Recent British General Election " and Sung Chiao-jen's translation of Ōsugi Sakae's article "Brief History of the Socialist International." Even more conspicuous, perhaps, was the absence of any discussion of the concept of the dialectical process of social development. Neither the term for "dialectics"--pien-cheng-fa coming from Japanese benshōhō--nor the terms for "materialism" (wei-wu-lun, yuibutsuron) or "materialistic conception of history" (wei-wu shih-kuan, yuibutsushikan) appeared in the documents analyzed. This seems to suggest that from the beginning the Chinese were attracted more by the practical than the theoretical apsect of Marxism. Throughout the 1920s, the classic for the Chinese Communists was the ABC of Communism by Nikolai Bukharin and Yevgeny A. Preobrazhensky.[75] Even Ch'ü Ch'iu-pai, who was regarded as a leading party "theoretician," confessed that he lacked a thorough grounding in Marx's writings.[76] The real significance of this fact is open to debate, for it is premature to arrive at any conclusion before a thorough study of the history of Chinese Marxism has been made. It is hoped, however, that the present paper may have provided, in a small measure, some useful background information for those intending to make either a general survey of socialism in China, the Chinese Communist movement, or a particular appraisal of Maoism.

# Notes

1. "On People's Democratic Dictatorship," Selected Works of Mao Tse-tung, New York: International Publishers, Vol. V, p. 413.

2. For example, on 28 February 1890 the North China Herald carried an article entitled "Socialism in Germany." It reported the rising influence of the Social Democrats in the Parliament and attributed the ferment of socialism to Germany's poverty and increase of industrial workers. I am grateful to Mr. Chang Yü-fa for calling my attention to this item.

3. See Nan-yang hsüeh-hui yen-chiu tsu, comp., Yen Chi-tao hsien-sheng i-chu (Mr. Yen Chi-tao's Works), Singapore: Nan-yang hsüeh-hui, 1959, p. 109.

4. Kung-chuan Hsiao, "In and Out of Utopia: K'ang Yu-wei's Social Thought, II. Road to Utopia," Chung Chi Journal, Vol. 7, No. 2, May 1968, p. 109. Professor Hsiao has devoted a good many years to studying K'ang Yu-wei's philosophy, and his monographs are the most thorough and penetrating treatment of the subject: "K'ang Yu-wei and Confucianism," Monumenta Serica, Vol. XVIII, 1959; "The Philosophical Thought of K'ang Yu-wei: An Attempt at a New Synthesis," Monumenta Serica, Vol. XXI, 1962; "The Case for Constitutional Monarchy: K'ang Yu-wei's Plan for Democratization of China," Monumenta Serica, Vol. XXIV, 1965; "In and Out of Utopia: K'ang Yu-wei's Social Thought, I. Path Finding

in Two Worlds," Chung-chi Journal, Vol 7, No. 1, November 1967; "K'ang Yu-wei's Excursion into Science: Lectures on the Heavens," reprinted in K'ang Yu-wei: A Biography and Symposium, edited with introduction by Jung-pang Lo, No. XXIII, Monographs of the Association for Asian Studies, The University of Arizona Press, 1967.

5. "In and Out of Utopia, II," op. cit., p. 111 and p. 139, fn. 67. See also Laurence G. Thomson, tr., Ta T'ung Shu: The One-World Philosophy of K'ang Yu-wei, London, 1958, p. 228, fn. 6.

6. "In and Out of Utopia, II," op. cit., p. 109.

7. Ibid.

8. Thompson, op. cit., p. 211.

9. "In and Out of Utopia, II," op. cit., p. 109.

10. Ibid., p. 128.    11. Ibid., p. 109.

12. Ibid., p. 126.    13. Ibid., p. 109.

14. Ibid., pp. 128, 125. I am grateful to Professor Kung-chuan Hsiao for his kindness in answering my question regarding K'ang Yu-wei's socialism.

15. "In and Out of Utopia, I," op. cit., p. 2; "In and Out of Utopia, II," op. cit., p. 121.

16. Robert A. Scalapino and Harold Schiffrin, "Early Socialist Currents in the Chinese Revolutionary Movement: Sun Yat-sen versus Liang Ch'i-ch'ao," Journal of Asian Studies, Vol. XVIII, No. 3, May 1959, p. 335.

17. Ch'ing-i pao, No. 31, published on 25 October 1899. See also Jung Meng-yüan, "Hsin-hai ke-ming ch'ien Chung-kuo shu-k'an shang tui Ma-k'e-ssu chu-i ti chieh-shao (The Introduction of Marxism in Chinese Publications Before the Revolution of 1911), Hsin chien-she, March 1953. Jung's source is Yin-ping shih wen-chi, "Chi-hai chi," Shanghai: Kuang-chih shu-chü, 1903, p. 41. This particular essay is not included in the 1960 edition of Yin-ping shih wen-chi reprinted by the Chung-hua Bookstore in Taiwan, which I have used.

18. Ting Wen-chiang, Liang Jen-kung hsien-sheng nien-p'u ch'ang-pien, ch'u-kao (Draft Chronological Biography of Liang Ch'i-ch'ao), 3 vols., Taipei: Shih-chieh shu-chü, 1958, Vol. 1, p. 94.

19. Sanetō Keishū, Chūgokujin Nihon ryūgaku shi (History of Chinese Students in Japan), Tokyo: Kuroshio, 1960, p. 343.

20. Ibid., p. 341; and P'eng Wen-tsu, Man-jen hsia-ma ti hsin ming-tz'u, Tokyo, 1915, pp. 10-11.

21. Yin-ping shih tzu-yu shu, Taipei: Chung-hua shu-chü, 1960, pp. 86-87.

114

22. Yin-ping shih wen-chi, Vol. 5, pp. 78-86.

23. "Erh-shih shih-chi chih chü-ling to-la-ssu," written under the pen name Chung-kuo chih hsin-min, Hsin-min ts'ung-pao, No. 42-43, p. 107.

24. Hsin-min ts'ung-pao, No. 46-48, published on 14 February 1904. See also Tzu-yu shu, pp. 101-102.

25. Hsin-min ts'ung-pao, No. 52, 10 September 1904; No. 53, 24 September 1904; No. 54, 9 October 1904; No. 56, 7 November 1904. See also Yin-ping shih wen-chi, Vol. 6, pp. 61-90.

26. Ting Wen-chiang, op. cit., Vol. 1, p. 147. The constitutionalists led by K'ang Yu-wei and Liang Ch'i-ch'ao played an important role in the development of modern Chinese journalism. Considering the introduction of new knowledge an essential means to promote reforms, they founded and ran several widely read journals at the turn of the century, such as the Shih-wu pao of Shanghai (Chinese Progress, 1896-1898), the Hsiang-hsüeh pao of Changsha (Hunanese Learning, 1897-1898), the Chih-hsin pao of Macao (Reformer China, 1897-1898), the Ch'ing-i pao of Yokohama (China Discussion, 1899-1901), the Hsin-min ts'ung-pao of Yokohama (New People's Miscellany, 1902-1907), the Cheng-lun (Political Discussion, 1907-1908, founded in Tokyo but later moved to Shanghai), and the Kuo-feng pao of Shanghai (National Trends, 1910-1911). They

115

also owned several newspapers, for example, the Shang pao of Hong Kong (Commercial Newspaper), the Hsin Chung-kuo pao of Honolulu (New China Newspaper), and Wen-hsing pao of San Francisco (Literature Prosperity Newspaper). The Extension of Knowledge Book Company was designed to further their influence and became in fact the distribution center for the constitutionalists' publications in mainland China. One of the few modern publishing firms in the late Ch'ing, the Company published numerous school textbooks and works on social and political science. One of its main features was translation, particularly Japanese works. Though the Company's publications sold well, poor management led to deficit and eventual bankruptcy in 1915. Thanks are due to Mr. Chang P'eng-yüan of Academia Sinica in Taiwan for providing some of the information on the Book Company. Mr. Chang intends to publish an article on the Company in the near future.

27. Chang Ching-lu, Chung-kuo chin-tai ch'u-pan shih-liao (Historical Materials on Modern Chinese Publishing), 2 vols., Shanghai: Ch'ün-lien ch'u-pan she, 1953-1954, Vol. 1, p. 174.

28. A copy of the second book, She-hui-tang, is available at the library of the University of California at Berkeley.

29. Jung Meng-yüan, op. cit., pp. 5-6.

30. Chung-kuo chin-tai ch'u-pan shih-liao,

Vol. 1, p. 174. Wang Te-chao, "T'ung meng Hui shih-ch'i Sun Chung-shan hsien-sheng ke-ming ssu-hsiang ti fen-hsi yen-chiu" (An Analytical Study of Sun Yat-sen's Thought during the T'ung-meng Hui Period), in Chung-kuo hsien-tai-shih ts'ung-k'an, edited by Wu Hsiang-hsiang, Taipei: Cheng-chung Bookstore, 1960, Vol. 1, pp. 182, 186. Wang says that an advertisement of Murai's book appeared in the Su pao on 12 November 1902, but he does not indicate the translator's name. This particular issue of the Su pao is unavailable in the U.S. The Su pao reprinted by the Kuomintang Archives in 1968 covers only the period from 6 May 1903 to 7 September 1903. The Su pao reprinted by the Hsüeh-sheng Bookstore in Taipei in 1965 covers the period from 27 February 1903 to 26 May 1903.

31. Shih-wu pao, No. 6, 27 September 1896.

32. Shih-wu pao, No. 50, 19 January 1898.

33. Four issues of the I-shu hui-pien are extant (1,2,7,8). The eighth issue appeared on 28 August 1901. It is not known how many issues were published afterwards. In 1903, the I-shu hui-pien was re-named Cheng-fa hsüeh-pao (Journal of Government and Law). The four issues reprinted by the Hsüeh-sheng Book Company in Taipei in 1961 are incomplete, with many pages

missing. For the part discussed here in the article by Ariga Nagao, see issue 1, 5 December 1900; and issue 2, 23 January 1901.

34. Wang Te-chao, op. cit., pp. 182, 186ff.

35. The Hsin-min ts'ung-pao was the most popular journal in mainland China at the time and Liang's Yin-ping shih tzu-yu shu was very much in demand. See Chang Ching-lu, Chung-kuo hsien-tai ch'u-pan shih-liao (Historical Materials on Contemporary Chinese Publishing), 5 Vols., Peking: Chung-hua shu-chü, 1954-1959, Vol. 1, pp. 390-391.

36. "The Triumph of Anarchism over Marxism, 1906-1907," in China in Revolution, the First Phase, 1900-1913, edited by Mary Clabaugh Wright, New Haven and London: Yale University Press, 1968, pp. 97-98.

37. Chung-kuo chin-tai ch'u-pan shih-liao, op. cit., Vol. 1, p. 174.

38. Harold Z. Schiffrin, Sun Yat-sen and the Origins of the Chinese Revolution, Berkeley and Los Angeles: University of California Press, 1968, pp. 283-293.

39. Wang Te-chao, op. cit., pp. 182, 186 ff. Wang's source is the Su pao, 20 November 1902.

40. Chang P'eng-yüan, Liang Ch'i-ch'ao yü Ch'ing-chi ke-ming (Liang Ch'i-ch'ao and the Revolution in the Late Ch'ing), Taipei: Academia Sinica, 1964, p. 242.

41. Ibid., pp. 242-243.

42. Jung Meng-yüan, op. cit., p. 10; Schiffrin, Sun Yat-sen, pp. 307-309. The Chih-kung-t'ang was the Triad Society; see ibid., p. 326.

43. Scalapino and Schiffrin, op. cit., p. 333.

44. Released on 26 November 1905 and 5 April 1906.

45. No. 5, published on 26 June 1906. For a detailed analysis of this article, see Scalapino and Schiffrin, op. cit., pp. 329-333.

46. No. 3, 5 April 1906.

47. No. 4, 1 May 1906.

48. For a biographical sketch of Chu Chih-hsin, see Howard L. Boorman, ed., Biographical Dictionary of Republican China, New York and London: Columbia University Press, 1967, Vol. 1, pp. 440-443. For a brief history of the Fa-cheng shu-ch'eng k'o, see Sanetō Keishū, op. cit., p. 71. No. 46-48 of the Hsin-min ts'ung-pao carried a detailed description of the Fa-cheng shu-ch'eng

k'o, providing information on its curriculum, tuition, and other school regulations. In his later years, Chu Chih-hsin learned to read English and Russian; see Ke-ming hsien-lieh hsien-chin chuan (Biographies of Revolution-ary Martyrs and Pioneers), pp. 428-451, in the collection Kuo-fu pai-nien tan-ch'en chi-nien ts'ung-shu (Collected Works in Celebration of the Centenary of the Birth of Our National Father), Taipei, 1965.

49. Scalapino and Schiffrin, op. cit., p. 333; Martin Bernal, op. cit., p.112.

50. Martin Bernal, op. cit., pp. 98-99. For background information on the early Japanese communist movement, see also George M. Beckmann and Okubo Genji, The Japanese Communist Party, 1922-1945, Stanford: Stanford University Press, 1969, pp. 1-11.

51. Scalapino and Schiffrin, op. cit., p. 333.

52. No. 3, 5 April 1906.

53. No. 12, 6 March 1907.

54. No. 86, 3 September 1906. As Scalapino and Schiffrin have pointed out: "This issue was apparently predated since it refers to Sun's speech of October"; op.cit., p. 335. In fact, the Hsin-min ts'ung-pao frequently predated its publication.

55. Nos. 90-92, published on 1 November 1906, 16 November 1906, and 30 November 1906.

56. Published 14 February 1904.

57. Wu Chung-yao was a younger brother of Wu T'ieh-ch'iao, a close friend of Liang Ch'i-ch'ao in Liang's youth. In the early 20th century Wu Chung-yao attended a Japanese college with Liang's support and was a frequent contributor to the Hsin-min ts'ung-pao. Wu was a member of the Cheng-wen She (Society of Political Information), which Liang organized in 1907. During the early Republican period, Wu continued to be Liang's political follower. Thanks are extended here to Mr. Chang P'eng-yüan for his kindness in providing me the information on Wu Chung-yao.

58. Published on 1 May 1906.

59. Biographical Dictionary of Republican China, Vol. II, pp. 30-31.

60. Published on 30 June 1906.

61. Published on 5 September 1907.

62. No. 2, 26 November 1905.

63. No. 4, 1 May 1906.

64. Jung Meng-yüan, op. cit., p. 10.

121

65. Li Shu, <u>Chin-tai shih lun-ts'ung</u> (Collected Essays on Modern History), Peking: Hsüeh-hsi tsa-chih che, 1956, p. 14.

66. For example, "Wu-cheng-fu chu-i chih liang-p'ai" (Two Factions of the Anarchists), No. 8, 8 October 1906; "Hsü-wu-tang hsiao-shih" (A Short History of the Anarchists), Nos. 11 and 17, 30 January 1907 and 25 October 1907; "Su-fei-ya chuan" (A Biography of Sophia), No. 15, 5 July 1907; and "Pa-ku-ning chuan" (A Biography of Bakunin), No. 16, 25 September 1907. For a listing of articles on anarchism published in the <u>Min-pao</u>, see Martin Bernal, <u>op. cit.</u>, p. 135.

67. See also Sanetō Keishū, <u>op. cit.</u>, pp. 333-408; Wang Li-ta, "Hsien-tai Han-yü chung ts'ung Jih-yü chieh-lai te tz'u-hui" (Modern Chinese Terms of Japanese Origin), <u>Chung-kuo yü-wen</u>, Peking, No. 68, February 1958, pp. 90-94; Cheng Tien, "T'an hsien-tai Han-yü chung te 'Jih-yü yü-hui'" (On Japanese Terms in the Modern Chinese Language), <u>Chung-kuo yü-wen</u>, No. 68, pp. 94-95; Chang Ying-te, "Hsien-tai Han-yü chung neng yu che-mo to te Jih-yü chieh-tz'u ma" (Are There So Many Modern Chinese Terms Borrowed from Japanese?), <u>Chung-kuo yü-wen</u>, No. 72, June 1958, p. 299; Shao Jung-fen, "P'ing 'Hsien-tai Han-yü wai-lai-tz'u yen-chiu'" (On A Study of Terms of Foreign Origin in Modern Chinese

Language), <u>Chung-kuo yü-wen</u>, No. 73,
July 1958, pp. 347-348.

68. Sources conflict on the numbers of
Chinese students in Japan. The figure
given in the text is based on Sanetō
Keishū, <u>op. cit.</u>, p. 58. "The <u>Japan
Chronicle</u> reports that by 1905 their
numbers had reached nearly 3,000,
9,000 in 1906, and 13,000 two or three
years later, before the tide began to
subside." See Joseph R. Levenson, <u>Liang
Ch'i-ch'ao and the Mind of Modern China</u>,
Cambridge: Harvard University Press, 1959,
p. 81. On the books translated from
the Japanese. See <u>Chung-kuo chin-tai
ch'u-pan shih-liao</u>, <u>op. cit.</u>, II, pp.
95-101.

69. These are <u>Hsin erh-ya</u>, compiled by
Wang Jung-pao and Yeh Lan, Shanghai:
Ming-ch'üan she, printed in Tokyo, 1903;
<u>Han i hsin fa-lüeh tz'u-tien</u>, by Chang
Chi-kuang and Hsü Yung-hsi, printed in
Tokyo, 1905; <u>Jih-pen fa-kuei chieh-tzu</u>,
by Ch'ien Hsün and Tung Hung-wei,
Shanghai, 1907; Huang Mo-hsi, <u>P'u-
t'ung pao-k'e hsin ta tz'u-tien</u>, Chung-
kuo tz'u-tien kung-ssu, 1911; and others.
See Sanetō Keishū, <u>op. cit.</u>, pp. 347-
353.

70. Kao Ming-k'ai and Liu Cheng-tan, <u>op.
cit.</u>, pp. 3, 80-81.

71. I have a list of Chinese students in
Russia at the turn of the century and
intend to publish it in the future.

72. My interviews with more than a dozen
people who were involved in Russian
affairs during the 1920s and 1930s.
They used Russian-Japanese dictionaries.

73. See Li Ti-hsün, "P'ing Kuo pien O-Hua
tz'u-tien" (On the Russian-Chinese
Dictionary by Kuo), Fan-i t'ung-pao,
March 1952.

74. See Ch'ü Ch'iu-pai, Chung-kuo ke-ming
yü kung-ch'an-tang (The Chinese Revolution and the Communist Party), Moscow,
1928, pp. 83-84.

75. My interviews with more than twenty
persons who were involved in the Chinese
Communist movement in the 1920s and
1930s.

76. "To yü te hua" (Superfluous Words),
I-ching, No. 26, 20 March 1935, p. 18.

## Glossary

| | |
|---|---|
| Ariga Nagao | 有賀長雄 |
| Chao Pi-chen | 趙必振 |
| Cheng-fa hsüeh-pao | 政法學報 |
| Chia-lu Ma-lu-k'o-ssu | 加陸馬陸科斯 |
| Chih-kung-t'ang | 致公堂 |
| Chin-hua-lun ke-ming-che chi-te chih hsüeh-shuo | 進化論革命者頡德之學說 |
| Chin-shih cheng-chih shih | 近世政治史 |
| ch'u-kou | 芻狗 |
| chün-ch'an chih shuo | 均產之說 |
| chün-fu chih shuo | 均富之說 |
| chün p'in-fu chih tang | 均貧富之黨 |
| ch'ün hsüeh | 群學 |
| Chung-kuo chih she-hui chu-i | 中國之社會主義 |
| Chung-kuo jih-pao | 中國日報 |
| Erh-shih shih-chi chih kuai-wu ti-kuo chu-i | 二十世紀之怪物帝國主義 |

Fa-cheng su-ch'eng k'o 法政速成科

fu-shen 富紳

hao-yu 豪右

Hikaku zaiseigaku 比較財政學

Hisamatsu Yoshinori 久松義典

Hou T'ai-wan 侯太綰

hsi-min 細民

Hsin shih-chieh
  hsüeh-pao 新世界學報

Huang Tsun-hsien 黃遵憲

I-shu hui-pien she 譯書彙編社

i-ti 邑地

jen-ch'ün chih shuo 人群之說

Junkō 巡耕

Kakakunō zaiseigaku 華格納財政學

Kinsei shakai shugi
  hyoron 近世社會主義評論

kan-she yü fang-jen 干涉與放任

K'ang Yu-wei 康有為

Kawakami Hajime 河上肇

| | |
|---|---|
| Keizaigaku gairon | 經濟學概論 |
| Kobayashi Usaburō | 小林丑三郎 |
| Kokka gakkai zasshi | 國家學會雜誌 |
| Kokumin shimpō | 國民新報 |
| Kōtō sozei genron | 高等租稅原論 |
| Kōtoku shūsui | 幸德秋水 |
| Kuang-chih shu-chü | 廣智書局 |
| kuo-ch'an chu-i | 國產主義 |
| La-shih-so-erh | 拉士梭爾 |
| La-ssu-lai | 拉司來 |
| lao-min | 勞民 |
| Lun ch'iang-ch'üan | 論強權 |
| Ma-erh-k'e | 馬爾克 |
| Mai-k'e-shih | 麥喀士 |
| Mai-k'e-ssu | 麥克司 |
| min-chu chuan-cheng | 民主專政 |
| min-tang | 民黨 |
| Miyazaki Tamizō | 宮崎民藏 |
| Murai Chishi | 村井知至 |

127

| | |
|---|---|
| Nan-yang Kung-hsüeh | 南洋公學 |
| Nishikawa Kōjirō | 西川光次郎 |
| pien-cheng fa | 辯證法 |
| p'ing-min | 平民 |
| Sakai Toshihiko | 堺利彦 |
| She-hui chu-i kai-p'ing | 社會主義概評 |
| shih-chieh chih kung-li | 世界之公理 |
| Shimada Saburō | 島田三郎 |
| Su Hsün | 蘇洵 |
| Su pao | 蘇報 |
| Ta-t'ung shu | 大同書 |
| Takimoto Yoshio | 瀧本美夫 |
| Tanaka Hozumi | 田中穗積 |
| Tu Shih-chen | 杜士珍 |
| tzu-yu | 自由 |
| tzu-yu-ti | 自由地 |
| Ukita Kazuomi | 浮田和民 |

| | |
|---|---|
| wai-tzu shu-ju wen-t'i | 外資輸入問題 |
| Wan-kuo kung-jen tsung-hui | 萬國工人總會 |
| wan-kuo ta-hui | 萬國大會 |
| Wang An-shih | 王安石 |
| Wang K'ang-nien | 汪康年 |
| Wang Mang | 王莽 |
| wei-wu lun | 唯物論 |
| wei-wu shih-kuan | 唯物史觀 |
| Wu T'ieh-ch'iao | 吳鉄樵 |
| Yamauchi Masaki | 山内正瞭 |
| yeh-ti | 野地 |
| Yen-chi-erh | 嫣及爾 |
| Yen Fu | 嚴復 |
| yu-chu-ti | 有主地 |
| yüan ch'iang | 原強 |
| yüan-man | 圓滿 |

# Bibliography

Beckmann, George M. and Genji, Okubo.
The Japanese Communist Party, 1922-
1945. Stanford: Stanford University
Press, 1969.

Bernal, Martin. "The Triumph of
Anarchism over Marxism, 1906-1907,"
in China in Revolution, edited by
Mary Clabaugh Wright. New Haven and
London: Yale University Press, 1968.

Boorman, Howard L. Biographical Dictionary of Republican China, Vol. 1
and Vol. 2. New York and London:
Columbia University Press, 1967-1968.

Chang  Ching-lu 張靜廬. Chung-kuo
chin-tai ch'u-pan shih-liao
中國近代出版史料
(Historical Materials on Modern
Chinese Publishing). 2 Vols.
Shanghai: Ch'ün-lien ch'u-pan she,
1953-54.

_____. Chung-kuo hsien-tai ch'u-
pan shih-liao 中國現代出版史料
(Historical Materials on Contemporary Chinese Publishing). 5 Vols.
Peking: Chung-hua shu-chü, 1954-1959.

Chang  P'eng-yüan 張朋園 . Liang Ch'i-
ch'ao yü Ch'ing-chi ke-ming
梁啟超與清季革命
(Liang Ch'i-ch'ao and the Revolution

in the Late Ch'ing). Taipei: Academia Sinica, 1964.

Chang Ying-te 張應德 . "Hsien-tai Han-yü chung neng-yu che-mo to te Jih-yü chieh-tz'u ma" 現代漢語中能有這麼多的日語借詞嗎 (Can There Be So Many Modern Chinese Terms of Japanese Origin?), Chung-kuo yü-wen 中國語文 , No. 72, June 1958.

Cheng Tien 鄭奠 . "T'an hsien-tai Han-yü chung te 'Jih-yü yü-hui'" 談現代漢語中的日語語彙 (On Japanese Terms in the Modern Chinese Language), Chung-kuo yü-wen, No. 68, February 1958.

Chu Chih-hsin 朱執信 (under the pen name Hsien-chieh 縣解 ). "Lun she-hui ke-ming tang yü cheng-chih ke-ming ping-Hsing" 論社會革命當與政治革命並行 (Why the Social Revolution Should Be Carried Out Simultaneously with the Political Revolution), Min-pao, No. 5, 26 June 1906.

——————— (under the pen name Che-shen 蟄伸 ). "Te-i-chih she-hui ke-ming-chia hsiao-chuan" 德意志社會革命家小傳 (Short Biographies of German Social Revolutionaries), Min-pao, No. 2, 26 November 1905, and No. 3, 5 April 1906.

_____ (under the pen name Hsien-chieh 縣解). "Ts'ung she-hui chu-i lun t'ieh-tao kuo-yu chi Chung-kuo t'ieh-tao chih kuan-pan ssu-pan" 從社會主義論鉄道國有及中國鉄道之官辦私辦 (Discussion from a Socialist Viewpoint of Railway Nationalization and Official and Private Management of China's Railways), Min-pao, No. 4, 1 May 1906.

_____ (under the pen name Che-shen 蟄伸). "Ying-kuo hsin tsung-hsüan-chü lao-tung-che chih chin-pu" 英國新總選舉勞動者之進步 (The Progress of the Proletariat in the Recent British General Election), Min-pao, No. 3, 5 April 1906.

Ch'ü Ch'iu-pai 瞿秋白. Chung-kuo ke-ming yü kung-ch'an-tang 中國革命與共產黨 (The Chinese Revolution and the Communist Party). Moscow, 1928.

_____. "To yü te hua" 多餘的話 (Superfluous Words), I-ching 逸經, No. 26, 20 March 1935.

Chung-kuo kuo-min-tang chung-yang tang-shih shih-liao pien-tsuan wei-yüan-hui 中國國民黨中央黨史史料編纂委員會 Kuo-fu pai-nien tan-ch'en chi-nien ts'ung-shu 國父百年誕辰紀念叢書 (Collected Works in Celebration of

the Centenary of the Birth of Our
National Father). Taipei, 1965.

Feng  Tzu-yu 馮自由  (under the name
    Tzu-yu 自由 ).  "Min-sheng chu-i yü
    Chung-kuo cheng-chih ke-ming chih
    ch'ien-t'u"民生主義與中國政治革命之前途
    (The Min-sheng Principle and the
    Future of the Chinese Political
    Revolution), <u>Min-pao</u>, No. 4, 1 May 1906.

Hsiao, Kung-chuan. "In and out of Utopia:
    K'ang Yu-wei's Social Thought, I.
    Path Finding in Two Worlds," <u>The
    Chung-chi Journal</u>, Vol. 7, No. 1,
    November 1967.

_____. "In and out of Utopia:
    K'ang Yu-wei's Social Thought, II.
    Road to Utopia," <u>The Chung-chi
    Journal</u>, Vol. 7, No. 2, May 1968.

Hu Han-min 胡漢民 (under the pen name
    Min-i 民意 ).  "Kao fei-nan min-
    sheng chu-i che" 告非難民生主義者
    (To the Critic of the <u>Min-sheng</u> chu-i),
    <u>Min-pao</u>, No. 12, 6 March 1907.

_____ (under the name Han-min
    漢民 ).  "Min-pao chih liu-ta chu-i"
    民報之六大主義     (The Six Great
    Principles of the <u>Min-pao</u>), <u>Min-pao</u>,
    No. 3, 5 April 1906.

<u>I-shu hui-pien</u> 譯書彙編  .  Reprinted
    by the Hsüeh-sheng Book Company in
    Taipei, 1961.

Jung Meng-yüan 榮孟源 . "Hsin-hai ke-ming ch'ien Chung-kuo shu-k'an shang tui Ma-k'e-ssu chu-i te chieh-shao" 辛亥革命前中國書刊上對馬克思主義的介紹 (The Introduction of Marxism in Chinese Publications before the Revolution of 1911), <u>Hsin chien-she</u> 新建設 March 1953.

Kao Ming-k'ai 高名凱 and Liu Cheng-tan 劉正琰 . <u>Hsien-tai Han-yü wai-lai-tz'u yen-chiu</u> 現代漢語外來詞研究 (A Study of Terms of Foreign Origin in the Modern Chinese Language). Peking: Wen-tzu kai-ke ch'u-pan she, 1958.

Levenson, Joseph R. <u>Liang Ch'i-ch'ao and the Mind of Modern China</u>. Cambridge: Harvard University Press, 1959.

Li Shu 黎澍 . <u>Chin-tai shih lun-ts'ung</u> 近代史論叢 Collected Essays on Modern History). Peking: Hsüeh-hsi tsa-chih she, 1956.

Li Ti-hsün 李迪勳 . "P'ing Kuo pien O-Hua tz'u-tien" 評郭編俄華辭典 (On the Russian-Chinese Dictionary by Kuo), <u>Fan-i t'ung-pao</u> 翻譯通報 March 1952.

Liang Ch'i-ch'ao 梁啟超 . <u>Yin-ping shih wen-chi</u> 飲冰室文集 Taipei: Chung-hua shu-chü, 1960.

_____ (under the pen name Yin-ping 飲冰). "Tsa-ta mou-pao" 雜答某報 (Miscellaneous Answers to a Certain Paper), Hsin-min ts'ung-pao, Nos. 84-86, 4 August 1906, 24 August 1906, 3 September 1906.

_____. "Tsai po mou pao chih t'u-ti kuo-yu lun" 再駁某報之土地國有論 (A Further Refutation of a Certain Paper's Land Nationalization Doctrine), Hsin-min ts'ung-pao, Nos. 90-92, 1 November 1906, 16 November 1906, 30 November 1906.

Liao Chung-k'ai 廖仲凱 (under the pen name Yüan-shih 淵實). "She-hui chu-i shih ta-kang" 社會主義史大綱 (Outline History of Socialism), Min-pao, No. 7, 5 September 1907.

Mao Tse-tung. Selected Works of Mao Tse-tung. New York: International Publishers, 5 vols.

Nan-yang hsüeh-hui yen-chiu tsu 南洋學會研究組, comp. Yen Chi-tao hsien-sheng i-chu 嚴幾道先生遺著 (Yen Fu's Works). Singapore: Nan-yang hsüeh-hui, 1959.

P'eng Wen-tsu 彭文祖. Mang-jen hsia-ma ti hsin ming-tz'u 盲人瞎馬的新名詞. Tokyo, 1915.

Sanetō Keishū 實藤惠秀. Chūgokujin Nihon ryūgaku shi 中國人留學日本史 (History of Chinese Students in Japan). Tokyo: Kuroshio, 1960.

Scalapino, Robert A., and Schiffrin,
    Harold.  "Early Socialist Currents
    in the Chinese Revolutionary Move-
    ment: Sun Yat-sen versus Liang Ch'i-
    ch'ao," Journal of Asian Studies,
    Vol. XVIII, No. 3, May 1959.

Schiffrin, Harold Z.  Sun Yat-sen and
    the Origins of the Chinese Revolution.
    Berkeley and Los Angeles: University
    of California Press, 1968.

Shao  Jung-fen 邵榮芬.  "P'ing 'Hsien-
    tai Han-yü wai-lai-tz'u yen-chiu'"
    評現代漢語外來詞研究
    (On A Study of Terms of Foreign
    Origin in Modern Chinese Language).
    Chung-kuo yü-wen 中國語文,
    No. 73, July 1958.

Shih-wu pao 時務報 .  Shanghai,
    1896-1898.

"Socialism in Germany," North China
    Herald, 28 February 1890.

Sung  Chiao-jen 宋教仁 (under the pen
    name Ch'iang-chai 强齋 ).  "Wan-kuo
    she-hui-tang ta-hui shih-lüeh"
    萬國社會黨大會史略
    (Brief History of the Socialist
    International), Min-pao, No. 5,
    30 June 1906.

Ting  Wen-chiang 丁文江.  Liang Jen-
    kung hsien-sheng nien-p'u ch'ang-

pien ch'u-kao 梁任公先生年譜
長編初稿 (Draft Chronological
Biography of Liang Ch'i-ch'ao). 3
Vols. Taipei: Shih-chieh shu-chü,
1958.

Thompson, Laurence G., tr. <u>Ta Tung Shu:</u>
<u>The One-World Philosophy of K'ang</u>
<u>Yu-wei</u>. London: George Allen and
Unwin Ltd., 1958.

"T'u-ti fu-ch'üan t'ung-chih-hui chu-i
shu"土地復權同志會主意書
(Program of the Society for the
Restoration of Land Rights), <u>Min-pao</u>
No. 2, 26 November 1905.

Wang Li-ta 王立達 . "Hsien-tai Han-
yü chung ts'ung Jih-yü chieh-lai ti
tz'u-hui"
現代漢語中從日語借來的詞彙
(Modern Chinese Terms of Japanese
Origin), <u>Chung-kuo yü-wen</u> 中國語文,
Peking, No. 68, February 1958.

Wang Te-chao王德昭 . "T'ung-meng Hui
shih-ch'i Sun Chung-shan hsien-
sheng ke-ming ssu-hsiang ti fen-hsi
yen-chiu 同盟會時期孫中山先生革命
思想的分析研究 (An Analytical Study
of Sun Yat-sen's Thought During the
T'ung-meng Hui Period), in Chung-kuo
hsien-tai shih ts'ung-k'an 中國現代史
叢刊 , ed. by Wu Hsiang-hsiang 吳相湘
Taipei: Cheng-chung Bookstore, 1960.

Wu Chung-yao 吳仲遙 . "She-hui chu-i
lun" 社會主義論 (A Discussion of

Socialism), <u>Hsin-min ts'ung-pao</u>, No. 89, 14 February 1904.

Yeh Hsia-sheng 葉夏生 (under the pen name Meng-tieh-sheng 夢蝶生 ). "Wu-cheng-fu tang yü ke-ming-tang chih shuo-ming" 無政府黨與革命黨之說明 (An Explanation of the Anarchist Parties and Revolutionary Parties), <u>Min-pao</u>, No. 7, 5 September 1907.

# PUBLICATIONS OF THE EAST ASIAN INSTITUTE

## STUDIES

*The Ladder of Success in Imperial China,*
  by Ping-ti Ho. New York: Columbia Uni-
  versity Press, 1962.
*The Chinese Inflation, 1937-1949,* by Shun-
  hsin Chou. New York: Columbia University Press, 1963.
*Reformer in Modern China: Chang Chien,*
  *1853-1926,* by Samuel Chu. New York:
  Columbia University Press, 1965.
*Research in Japanese Sources: A Guide,* by
  Herschel Webb with the assistance of
  Marleigh Ryan. New York: Columbia Uni-
  versity Press, 1965.
*Society and Education in Japan,* by Herbert
  Passin. New York: Bureau of Publica-
  tions, Teachers College, Columbia Uni-
  versity, 1965.
*Agricultural Production and Economic De-*
  *velopment in Japan, 1873-1922,* by James
  I. Nakamura. Princeton: Princeton Uni-
  versity Press, 1966.
*Japan's First Modern Novel: Ukigumo of*
  *Futabatei Shimei,* by Marleigh Ryan.
  New York: Columbia University Press,
  1967.
*The Korean Communist Movement, 1918-1948,*
  by Dae-Sook Suh. Princeton: Princeton
  University Press, 1967.
*The First Vietnam Crisis,* by Melvin Gurtov.
  New York: Columbia University Press,
  1967. Paperback edition, 1968.
*Cadres, Bureaucracy, and Political Power in*
  *Communist China,* by A. Doak Barnett.
  New York: Columbia University Press,
  1967.

*The Japanese Imperial Institution in the Tokugawa Period*, by Herschel Webb. New York: Columbia University Press, 1968.

*Higher Education and Business Recruitment in Japan*, by Koya Azumi. New York: Teachers College Press, Columbia University, 1969.

*The Communists and Chinese Peasant Rebellion: A Study in the Rewriting of Chinese History*, by James P. Harrison, Jr. New York: Atheneum Publishers, 1969.

*How the Conservatives Rule Japan*, by Nathaniel B. Thayer. Princeton: Princeton University Press, 1969.

*Aspects of Chinese Education*, edited by C.T. Hu. New York: Teachers College Press, Columbia University, 1969.

*Economic Development and the Labor Market in Japan*, by Koji Taira. New York: Columbia University Press, 1970.

*The Japanese Oligarchy and the Russo-Japanese War*, by Shumpei Okamoto. New York: Columbia University Press, 1970.

*Japanese Education: A Bibliography of Materials in the English Language*, by Herbert Passin. New York: Teachers College Press, Columbia University, 1970.

*Documents of Korean Communism, 1918-1948*, by Dae-Sook Suh. Princeton: Princeton University Press, 1970.

*Japan's Postwar Defense Policy, 1947-1968*, by Martin E. Weinstein. New York: Columbia University Press, 1971.

*Election Campaigning: Japanese Style*, by Gerald L. Curtis. New York: Columbia University Press, forthcoming.

*China and Russia: The "Great Game,"* by O. Edmund Clubb. New York: Columbia University Press, forthcoming.

*Imperial Restoration in Medieval Japan*, by
    H. Paul Varley. New York: Columbia Uni-
    versity Press, forthcoming.
*Li Tsung-jen: A Memoir*, edited by T.K.
    Tong. Berkeley: University of Califor-
    nia Press, forthcoming.
*Money and Monetary Policy in Communist
    China during the First Five Year Plan*,
    by Katharine H. Hsiao. New York: Co-
    lumbia University Press, forthcoming.
*Law and Policy in China's Foreign Rela-
    tions*, by James C. Hsiung. New York:
    Columbia University Press, forthcoming.


RESEARCH AIDS

*Sino-Japanese Relations, 1862-1927: A
    Checklist of the Chinese Foreign Min-
    istry Archives*, compiled by Kuo Ting-
    yee and edited by James W. Morley.
    New York: East Asian Institute, Colum-
    bia University, 1965.
*The Research Activities of the South Man-
    churian Railway Company, 1907-1945: A
    History and Bibliography*, by John
    Young. New York: East Asian Institute,
    Columbia University, 1966.
*Chinese Law Past and Present: A Bibliog-
    raphy of Enactments and Commentaries in
    English Text*, compiled and edited by
    Fu-shun Lin. New York: East Asian In-
    stitute, Columbia University, 1966.
*A Bibliography of Secondary English Lan-
    guage Literature on Contemporary Chi-
    nese Politics*, by Michel C. Oksenberg
    with Nancy Bateman and James B. Ander-
    son. New York: East Asian Institute,
    Columbia University, 1970.

*A Guide to British Foreign Office: Confidential Print: China, 1848-1922. Microfilm F.O. 405*, by Carol Reynolds. New York: East Asian Institute, Columbia University, 1970.


OCCASIONAL PAPERS

*Historians and American Far Eastern Policy*, compiled by Dorothy Borg. New York: East Asian Institute, Columbia University, 1966.

*Provincial Party Personnel in Mainland China, 1956-1966*, by Frederick C. Teiwes. New York: East Asian Institute, Columbia University, 1967.

*Reality and Illusion: The Hidden Crisis Between Japan and the U.S.S.R., 1932-1934*, by Ikuhiko Hata. New York: East Asian Institute, Columbia University, 1967.

*Imperial Japan and Asia: A Reassessment*, compiled by Grant K. Goodman. New York: East Asian Institute, Columbia University, 1967.

*American Presurrender Planning for Postwar Japan*, by Hugh Borton. New York: East Asian Institute, Columbia University, 1967.

*The Legacy of the Occupation--Japan*, by Herbert Passin. New York: East Asian Institute, Columbia University, 1968.

*Taiwan: Studies in Chinese Local History*, edited by Leonard H.D. Gordon. New York: Columbia University Press, 1970.

*The Introduction of Socialism into China*, by Li Yu-ning. New York: Columbia University Press, 1971.

*The Early Chiang Kai-shek: A Study of His Personality and Politics, 1887-1924*, by Pichon P.Y. Loh. New York: Columbia University Press, forthcoming.

REPRINTS

*The Communist Movement in China*, by Ch'en Kung-po, edited with an Introduction by C. Martin Wilbur. New York: Octagon Books, 1966.

*American Policy and the Chinese Revolution, 1925-1928*, by Dorothy Borg. New York: Octagon Books, 1968.

*The Fabric of Chinese Society*, by Morton H. Fried. New York: Octagon Books, 1970.